Growing a Growth Mindset

Growing a Growth Mindset

Unlocking Character Strengths through Children's Literature

Kevin Sheehan and Jessica Ryan

ROWMAN & LITTLEFIELD
Lanham • Boulder • New York • London

/

Published by Rowman & Littlefield
A wholly owned subsidiary of The Rowman & Littlefield Publishing Group, Inc.
4501 Forbes Boulevard, Suite 200, Lanham, Maryland 20706
www.rowman.com

Unit A, Whitacre Mews, 26–34 Stannary Street, London SE11 4AB

British Library Cataloguing in Publication Information Available

Library of Congress Cataloging-in-Publication Data Is Available

ISBN 978-1-4758-2472-8 (cloth : alk. paper)
ISBN 978-1-4758-2473-5 (paper : alk. paper)
ISBN 978-1-4758-2474-2 (electronic)

∞™ The paper used in this publication meets the minimum requirements of American
National Standard for Information Sciences—Permanence of Paper for Printed Library
Materials, ANSI/NISO Z39.48–1992.

Printed in the United States of America

In Memory of Shane Lopez,
This is the ripple that spread from your hope.
Without you, this book does not happen.

To Irene, Ryan, Dylan, and Casey,
You are the source of my hope, and
the fuel that feeds my grit.

—K.P.S.

To Danny, Summer, and Riley,
You inspire me, challenge me, and
always encourage me to *grow*.
Love you to the moon and back!

—J.A.R.

Contents

List of Tables

List of Figures

Foreword

Spreading Shane's Ripples of Hope

When I was asked to write the foreword for this innovative book, my first thought was that my mentor, friend, and colleague, the late Shane Lopez, should be writing this and not me. Tragically, for all of us, Shane passed away on July 23, 2016, so I inherited the honor of introducing this text to you. For those of you who did not have the pleasure of knowing Shane Lopez, I could begin professionally by saying that Shane, along with C.R. Snyder, is considered one of the main sources from which the hope literature grew. More personally, I would say that Shane not only researched hope theory, but he also lived it. In a well-cited call to arms, Shane urged all of us to spread *ripples of hope* on every day of our lives. Shane spread *ripples of hope* in every day of his life, and I know, because I was one of those ripples.

The ripples of hope that Shane spread into my life began when I was a graduate student. Lost in the research and just starting out, I e-mailed Shane one of my early documents on hope. Though we did not know each other, Shane responded in the most encouraging way and took the time to provide extensive feedback, later agreeing to serve as a dissertation committee member, though more than a few states separated us. Shane had an easy comfortable way about him that he shared with everyone, no matter what your status.

Although researchers are overwhelmed and busy, Shane was never too busy to talk, explain a point, or give the extra boost of encouragement that you needed but were too embarrassed to admit. Shane had a way of knowing what kinds of encouragement people needed, and he gave of himself freely to provide that support. Shane's belief was that everyone needed at least a handful of cheerleaders, and for many of us, Shane became our prime cheerleader. Why all this talk about Shane Lopez? Without his research, I don't believe we would still be talking about hope. More importantly, it is my belief that the hope research of Shane Lopez helped pave the way for new positive psychology constructs that followed. I believe, and I think the authors would agree, that this book would not currently be in your hands had it not been for the groundwork laid by Shane.

This brings me to the present. Shane's message that our role in life was to create and spread ripples of hope in others came full circle for me when I met Professor Kevin Sheehan early in his doctoral studies. Although new to positive psychology, Kevin had the intense desire to know what motivates people, especially those who have received very little motivational encouragement in their lives. Kevin worked with students that he believed had lost hope seeking to measure hope and grit in alternative school students and trying to uncover how hope impacted their achievement and happiness. Kevin not only researched these students but also stayed on even after the research, seeking to spread ripples of hope into their lives.

Demonstrating the viral power of ripples of hope, when Kevin taught Jessica Ryan in a positive summer psychology course, Jessica became the next ripple of hope. Jessica, a devoted elementary school teacher, wanted to address the inequity between students who realize their own potential compared to those who feel powerless in her classroom. Collaborating together, Kevin and Jessica sought a way to inject the rich concepts of positive psychology into the lives of children. What emerged from this partnership between college and classroom was an approach to make positive psychology accessible to students through children's literature stories, promoting concepts like hope, grit, mindset, character strengths, and happiness. Discussing characters that exemplify positive perceptions in stressful situations enabled students to approach these constructs in a more concrete way.

All too often, those in educational leadership expect teachers to take directly from jargon-filled research literature and apply this research seamlessly into children's lives. This book provides methods of application that can effectively integrate positive psychology into the lives of children. The inclusion of lesson plans and guiding questions supports the educator in highlighting key components and how they may be expressed in everyday ways. This approach makes the process one that teachers can undertake regardless of their background in psychology. These stories not only help facilitate the development of positive psychology understanding in the student, but are also Common Core compliant and easily integrate into a teacher's lesson plans.

The ripples of hope emanating from this book extend beyond the classroom to parents. Each lesson is designed to end with an interactive experience between the child and the parent. Generally, parents are focused only on the end results of their children's hard work, the payoff of success. Children are often raised with the innate belief that their success should arise from innate talent and not effort. Children routinely seek to make success look as easy and painless as possible to demonstrate that they are talented. Sharing when we struggled, when we messed up, or even when we failed is not common in our society. However, the necessity of failing well is vital if children are to develop more realistic attitudes about belief, effort, and success. Students need to get comfortable with mistakes and failure as the essential path to learning if they are to become hopeful and gritty. This book provides a beginning to share these understandings with children.

Coming back to full circle to the Shane's mission of spreading *ripples of hope*, the book that you have in your hands offers you the vehicle to spread hope in the lives of the children in your life. In closing, it must be acknowledged that not everyone is afforded the same supporting resources to create hope, which is why we can't do it all alone. Hopefully, you will have a few Kevins and Jessicas in your corner. I know that Shane Lopez will be looking down and cheering you on as you share the stories in this book to spread your own *ripples of hope*.

Sage Rose, PhD
Hofstra University

Preface

Ripples of hope have the power to build cultures of grit.

Kevin Sheehan

Each time a man stands up for an ideal, or acts to improve the lot of others, or strikes out against injustice, he sends forth a tiny ripple of hope, and crossing each other from a million different centers of energy and daring, these ripples build a current which can sweep down the mightiest walls of oppression and resistance.

Robert F. Kennedy, June 6, 1966

Hope is the belief that we can not only imagine our future but we also have the power to make our dreams of that imagined future come true. Shane Lopez not only preached this ideal to the world, but he also embodied this ideal for all of us. With Shane's passing this year, America lost its preeminent hope scholar, the lead researcher for the Gallup Poll, but, most tragically of all, a man who sent ripples of hope in the world every day of his life.

This book attempts to bring to life the mission that Robert Kennedy just described so eloquently that defined Shane's life. This book empowers teachers and parents with a tool to creating ripples of hope in their students. Without tools to achieve our dreams, our dreams are often merely wishful thinking.

Using the vehicle of children's literature, we hope to present you with a tool to create your own ripples of hope. When those ripples of hope take root, we hope to enable you to build a classroom community that becomes one that can be defined by grit. Grit, as defined by Angela Duckworth, is the passion for a goal that enables one to persevere through obstacles over time.

Although education today is preoccupied with imparting knowledge and skills, the elephant in the room is that many of students in our classrooms lack hope. There might be no condition that is more depressing and desperate in a child than that of hopelessness. When a child has lost hope in the belief that he or she can achieve, there is no magic educational prescription or program that will light the lamp of learning.

Theories and goals about the twenty-first-century learning benchmarks that drive education today are constantly being refined and defined with exciting new methods. Measurements are daily being more precisely delineated by quantitative standards and measurements. For students lacking in hope, none of these innovations or more precise measurements will bring about the desired achievement. Inspired by Shane Lopez's legacy, helping children to rediscover hope is the first charge of this book.

Shane's research from the Gallup Poll estimated that half of the students in America are hopeful and envision a future that is brightly colored by dreams that they believe within their power to bring to life through their will and energy. Tragically, the other half of American students are stuck or discouraged and lack the belief that they have either the ways or the will to achieve their life's goals.

The stories from children's literature and the embedded positive psychology constructs that follow will most certainly capture the imagination of the children you teach. More importantly, we believe that these stories have the power to change the direction of your students' lives. Research tells us that hope, the belief that you know the path necessary to achieve your goals and the will to carry out those ways, is malleable, borrowing from the name of the popular movie *Hope Floats*.

The really good news about hope is that it is not a genetic trait that individuals are born with, but is a way of thinking. If we can change an individual's way of thinking, we can change that individual's hope. Teachers have the power to alter the course of their students' lives by providing the experiences, tools, and attitudes to enable students to define *or redefine* their thinking about their future. Teachers are not the only ones imbued with this special power to create hope. In the words of Shane Lopez, it is the job of all of us to *make hope happen*.

The stories that follow and the lesson plans to discover the meanings of those stories have the power to create ripples of hope in your students that can transform their dreams into realities by opening up the world of belief in them. The belief about our goals, and our perseverance to achieve those goals, is what transforms our dreams and wishes into reality.

The power of belief is no better championed than in the research of Angela Duckworth on grit. America has fallen in love with the idea of *grit*, and rightly so. *Grit: Passion and Perseverance for Long Term Goals*, by Angela

Duckworth, sits on atop the best-seller list, and many feel that Duckworth may have found the answer to what ails American education.

Grit, the passion and perseverance to achieve long-term goals, a researched psychological construct pioneered by Angela Duckworth, is dramatically changing the conversation on what children really need in education to be successful. Although *grit* may certainly be at the root of success in education, it would be hard to imagine a child lacking *hope*, the ability to imagine a successful future, ever exhibiting the passion and perseverance for long-term goals necessary for grit. Hope is the first step in the path to grit.

If a child has lost the belief that he or she has control of his or her future, there can be no passion to persevere toward any goal. In fact, children lacking hope have often abandoned goals. Without hope, the ways or pathways to achieve goals are cloudy and uncertain. Without hope, children lack agency, the will to achieve dreamed-of goals. Grit, as desired and essential a trait as it is in determining success, becomes merely wishful thinking without a foundation of hope.

The ripples of hope that Shane Lopez called on all of us to create lay the foundation necessary for teachers to establish cultures of grit. When children are hopeful that their goals are possible, they can then develop the persistence needed to achieve those goals in the face of obstacles in their path. Gritty students view and believe that setbacks are merely diversions on their way to goal attainment.

What makes this research on self-belief and self-direction so immediately relevant to every teacher reading this book is that questions now taking center stage in education are asking whether America's focus on raising standards might be better directed at programs seeking to alter the belief system of learners than in constructing more challenging assessments. Making a more challenging assessment is not all that difficult. The real challenge is how to motivate students to meet those more rigorous standards.

What has emerged from this passionate dialogue on what will make children more successful is the question of whether educators and parents can actually instill in children any set of beliefs. We can teach *about* psychological constructs, but can we teach children to be more hopeful or grittier? Is it within the power of teachers to instill in anyone how they will think and react in response to life's challenges and questions?

Try telling your child what they should believe, and the difficulty in teaching anyone what or how to think becomes apparent. Objections of our children to our dictating how they should think have been experienced by all of us. Loudly, we have all heard the shared and screamed anthem, "You can't tell me how to think." Your children are right. Try as we might, we can't mandate how they, or anyone else for that matter, should think.

Our most basic and cherished natural right is the right to determine our own beliefs. This book makes no attempt to dictate how children should think, feel, or believe. The lessons that follow do not dictate what a child should believe, but rather offer a set of stories, experiences, and compelling questions that provide a platform for students to examine, determine, and refine their own beliefs.

The compendium of children's stories that follows requires that children come to their own conclusions on a set of questions that would equally challenge us as adults. Rather than a mandate on what to think in regard to those questions, the stories and lesson activities that follow *inform thinking* and require deep analysis from students. Most certainly, these compelling questions will be shared at the dinner table.

Although Duckworth is clear that the research does not yet exist to document the fact that we can teach grit or any other character trait, in an inspiring TED talk to educators in April 2013, Duckworth challenged all of us in education to get "gritty about getting our kids to be grittier." Duckworth exhorted us to explore and develop "our best ideas, intuitions *and be willing to fail,* in our attempts to getting our kids to be grittier." The vehicle of children's literature that follows is our answer to Duckworth's call to arms.

The chapters that make up this book have the power to share with students the path that leads to the desired and vaunted goal of *grit*. That path begins with a growth mindset, the belief that success is not an innate and inborn capacity, but a product of effort. Understanding and maintaining a growth mindset is a prerequisite if children are to develop hope, the belief that they possess the ways and the will to achieve their desired goals.

Grit, rising up from hope, focuses more specifically on persevering toward long-term goals in the face of adversity. A child's grit arises out of a deep passion for a goal that stands the test of time. Grit's magical powers enable individuals to persevere through obstacles that might make others crumble.

Passion for the goal becomes more powerful and unshakeable when born of the character strengths and affinities that define the individual. Students, disliking math, may struggle through math homework. It is perseverance and self-control, and not grit, that get the student through the dreaded homework assignment.

Grit is better defined by what life is calling us to do, driven by our strengths and interests. Grit includes hard work determination, and even struggle, but it is born of passion for the goal. If grit and not perseverance is the goal, student ownership and choice in the direction of their learning is paramount. The work of Paul Solarz featured in *Learn Like a Pirate* provides a blueprint that empowers even the youngest of learners to design their own learning directions and outcomes.

Happiness is integrated naturally in an individual's mindset, hope, and grit, but can also be its own end, distinct from goal pursuit successes or failures. It is hard to imagine an individual not experiencing success in meeting goals being all too happy, but happiness is defined in the stories as more than successful goal pursuit. Happiness is not nearly what happens to us as *our view on what happens to us*.

At this point, you are most probably drowning in the breadth and newness of this content as well as overwhelming in the proposed mission of changing children's lives. You are being confronted with a foreign jargon, and it might be natural to have a sense that you are not up to this task. Fear not. No one is going to ask you to pursue a doctorate in positive psychology to be fluent in this content and vocabulary.

Instead, our plan is to provide you with sets of three simple read-aloud books on the five areas of positive psychology discussed previously. Together with your students, you will uncover the emerging research on growth mindset, hope, grit, character strengths, and happiness rather than covering it.

All of us in education have painfully come to realize that trying to be anyone else other than yourself in a classroom results only in disaster. We also know that teaching content you are not familiar with is not a prescription for success. We are not planning to ask you to teach positive psychology in the words of the researchers that will be shared with you to begin each chapter.

One of our prime motivations in writing this book was that teachers needed a practical and doable way to share this emerging and life-changing research with students. Fearing that you might make that mistake of trying to teach a content that you are not versed in, we begin by making a promise to you. You need only read the stories to provide a platform to integrate this content into your students' lives.

The required strategy that you need to be fluent in is that of reading aloud to your students and discovering the deeper meaning that emerges from that reading. We have provided for you a plan to do just that on each story in the book. As you read this set of stories and move through the lessons, you and your students will uncover the hidden truths that shape the emerging research, not only on hope and grit, but also on mindset, character strengths, and happiness.

The excitement inspired by positive psychology research gripping the nation now is part of a revolution in positive psychology begun by Martin Seligman more than five decades ago. Positive psychology has expanded the paradigm of psychology beyond methodologies and insights dealing with individuals with serious deficits into discovery of the secrets of how all of us might live more satisfying lives.

When one truly understands this new and exploding field of positive psychology, it becomes apparent that the private conversations in our head that shape on our beliefs are not limited to *hope* or *grit* as stand-alone agents, but are the product of the entire related family of interacting and interrelated psychological constructs. The reason that five constructs are presented rather just sharing one in is that none of the constructs exists in our heads on its own as an isolated and independent psychological construct.

What will become clear as you and your students move through the stories is that the big ideas of positive psychology overlap and correlate as if they were a *family*. Your students will discover this overlap as they move through the stories and relate back to previous stories. When Duckworth issued the call for teachers to develop best practices on how to make students *grittier*, her goal, by necessity, could not be achieved without the entire family of positive psychology relatives coming along as part of the process.

The selected children's books have been organized in a way that allows the psychological constructs to build on one another in a planned sequence, but the books and lessons can be shared with students in any order or even as stand-alone lessons or read-alouds. Our field tests reveal that students will discover the connections between the constructs in any order that they move through the lessons.

The stories will create a shared language between you and your students that may appear surprisingly even in different disciplines throughout the year. This new vocabulary often arms students with ability to express deeper understanding and insights in writing and can even pop up in your student responses when greater stamina in STEAM (science, technology, engineering, art, mathematics) is required. A positive by-product of the readings and lessons is that your students will most certainly gain deeper self-knowledge and, hopefully, also greater self-belief.

The ultimate goal is not to teach about positive psychology but to create a climate that unlocks students' strengths and, in the process, grows a growth mindset. This will not be a one-lesson deal or even a three-lesson unit. Teaching one lesson or reading one story on *hope* or *grit* will not magically instill that construct as a part of a student's new and improved learning personality. The goal of this approach is not merely to create a shared vocabulary, but to become a set of understandings and beliefs that transform the value system and actions of the class.

The real work for teachers will be to use these lessons to build an *environment* that nurtures the constructs, rather than one that merely talks about them. This environment will arise only when students adopt the *beliefs in practice* and not in mastery of the vocabulary and understandings of the stories taught. The success of the learning that emanates from the stories will not be ultimately measured on a test of how well students master the basic understandings of positive psychology, but by the degree to which these understandings influence student behavior.

It would be foolish to believe that this environment can be constructed without the full support of parents. Parents must adopt and reinforce the values that will define this learning environment, if this culture is to flourish. It must be emphasized that this culture of effort can be built only on the extensions of the lessons that teach parents alongside children.

Lessons from children's literature contained in this book were developed by extraordinary teachers from across Long Island. In a type of collaborative approach, teachers have shared and field-tested these lessons in each other's classrooms. The books and research behind this selection of books emanated from a desire of these educators to make positive psychology a replicable reality in every classroom. The hope is that after reading and exploring these stories with your students, you will join that collaborative.

The application of children's literature to impart growth mindset, hope, grit, character strengths, and happiness offers a format that you can use tomorrow in the classroom or tonight in bedtime reading. The rationale for this book is that teachers and students cannot wait for the knowledge that is emerging in positive psychology research settings to move into the hearts and minds of students. Heeding Duckworth's call to arms, we must pursue our best ideas and not be afraid to fail in those pursuits.

Too many of our students will benefit from this research today and cannot wait for these experimental studies to define our practice. All of us, teachers and students, must learn to look on life's failures as beginnings and not endings. We, as teachers, cannot be afraid to fail, if we do not want our students to fear failure. With that in mind, this book is a challenge to you as educators and lovers of children to make your school a place where teachers come to learn alongside their students.

Begin by reading a children's book to your students or your child tomorrow and you can make Shane Lopez's dream a reality by creating *ripples of hope* in the children that you teach. Those *ripples of hope* emanating children's books also provide the energy needed to answer Duckworth's call to arms by providing a foundation that has the power to transform your classroom culture into a culture of passionate and resilient learners defined by their *grit*.

Acknowledgments

We would like to thank Molloy College and the entire Molloy College family for their support in providing the foundation and the forum that allowed this work to grow. We would especially like to thank Dr. Maureen Walsh, dean of the Division of Education, Dr. Joanne O' Brien, director of Graduate Education, and Dr. Linda Kraemer, director of Undergraduate Education, for their unwavering passion in seeking new ways to help children learn. Louis Cino, director of Continuing Education, started all of this by encouraging and nurturing the Molloy College positive psychology summer institutes that gave rise to this work. Thanks also to our tireless graduate assistant, Kelly Amarante, for completing a host of behind-the-scene tasks with a smile on her face. Molloy College's thirst for new knowledge provided the spark that ignited this book.

We would also like to thank Dr. Lucille Iconis, superintendent of the Massapequa School District, for piloting and pioneering many of the ideas that shape this book in her school district. Special thanks must go to Michael Draper, a magnet and a leader for students, who had the courage to pilot these stories with ninth graders. His fearless band of fellow health educators, including supervisor Denise Baldinger and Jay Savares, provided a laboratory for students to explore the conversations in their heads under the leadership of their principal, Patrick Di Clemente. We would be remiss not to mention the Senior Nation Student leaders who helped develop and organize that program for their fellow students. A special thank you goes out to those student leaders, Bradley Baldinger, Christopher Bacotti, Julianne Smith, Casey Sheehan, and Sarah Woods.

Special thanks must also go to Lucille McAssey, principal of Waverly Park School in Lynbrook School District, for taking a chance on someone who was in the right place at the right time, Jessica Ryan. Lucille lives the mission of the title of this book, growing a growth mindset, in her every action as principal. As a leader, Lucille has always allowed teachers to pursue passion projects, and this book is largely a result of that leadership and courage. Also, thank you to Dr. Melissa Burak, Lynbrook School District superintendent, for supporting the implementation of these positive psychology lessons in her extraordinary district.

We would also like to thank Jessica's hope creators at Waverly Park School, fellow teachers Shari Bowes, Amy Garfinkel, and Courtney Jacobs. The encouragement and thoughtful advice from those colleagues truly informed the book. These ladies piloted the lessons in their classroom and made growth mindset their mantra.

The origins of these book selections can be traced back to a tweet sent out by Massapequa's director of technology, Ed Kemnitzer. After an in-service positive psychology presentation to his middle school, Ed polled his Twitter World for books that might bring to life mindset, hope, and grit. The books rolled in, and aided by the wisdom and advice of Jo Ellen McCarthy, the selection of books that make up this anthology took shape.

Finally, a debt of gratitude is owed to the extraordinary children's literature authors, whose books provide indelible lessons for children on the power of mindset, hope, grit, character strengths, and happiness. Thank you. Research tells us that the lessons that are revealed by your stories will stay with their readers for life.

Part I

INTRODUCTION

The Why, How, and Where of Positive Psychology for Kids

Chapter 1

The Why

Teaching Children to Fail Well in a Trophy Culture

> Why do I now need to introduce new material into the content when I am already drowning in the new age of Common Standards?

Educators and parents need this book now more than ever, because childhood has changed. If individuals were lucky enough to be born before the age of Common Core, Facebook, and data-driven instruction, childhood was a time for young people to find a place in the world while meandering through some early successes and a good number of failures.

Looking back, most adults can now fondly laugh at the disasters endured, the confusion that pervaded, eventually discovering strengths and finding a place in the world. Early failures were seen as a natural part of growing up and, hopefully, experiences that were learned from that helped mold adult character and beliefs. Today, children are being raised in a trophy culture.

You don't believe that children today are trophies! Check Facebook tonight to learn of all the achievements of any friends' child. Pictures, videos, and even text messages find parents celebrating the glorious experiences and accomplishments of children on every social media platform known to man.

A child's immediate and unquestioned success has become societies' most sought-after trophy, as well as evidence and validation of successful parenting. Today's world has less patience for the natural trial and error of failure that is often a vital part of growing up *and learning*. A fellow professor from Stanford shared the fact that A- is the new C at Stanford. Every teacher reading this text can identify with this accelerated and intense pressure for high grades, *from parents even more than students*.

To amplify the pressure of this trophy culture on childhood, the declining world status of the United States as an educational superpower has brought in new waves of more rigorous evaluation beginning at the earliest ages. What makes little sense is that as increasingly challenging standards are adopted, the culture that children now inhabit is increasingly intolerant of failure in any form.

Today's society not only does not teach children to fail well, but it is also often intolerant of failing at all. Again, every teacher reading this indictment can validate this assentation with all too many frightening personal anecdotes. Linking the words *fail* and *well* creates a rush of cognitive dissonance, but it is the secret to meeting more rigorous challenges.

How can an individual fail and this experience of failing be something that the individual does well? The word *fail* has come to have only negative consequences. However, thinking back, most challenging things achieved in life are built on initial failure.

Think about catching a ball, riding a bike, or long division, and stored memories will reveal that each milestone came only after learning from early mistakes and failures. Failing well in those activities meant an individual overcame setbacks and learned. Mistakes are the essential building blocks of learning.

Although children are continually urged not to worry about grades and to just give a best possible effort, the dirty little secret that doing one's best does not hold a candle to succeeding, excelling, and, more dramatically in the highest form of excelling, to winning in our world today. If grades are not all that important, why are they instantaneously shared with parents on computer portals that make them visible on a minute-to-minute basis?

As a nation, we idolize champions, but we disdain second place. There seems to be little place in life today for failure. It is vital that children be taught that immediate success is not the way people live and learn in the real world. Setbacks are challenges that make individuals stronger. The current culture has transformed childhood into an apprenticeship, training for real life, rather than a period of self-discovery.

Childhood has become a time of evaluation and not learning. The intolerance of the world for the natural growth that is childhood is the reason that the instructional content that follows is vital. The transformation of childhood has taken a toll on parents, students, and children, even those children achieving the sought-after trophy status.

Think more for a moment about those children who experience the personal struggles, trials, and tribulations that are an essential part of learning and discovering identity. Obstacles and setbacks should be a natural part of discovering one's place in the world, but in this intense age of evaluation and competition, children experiencing failure may grow up believing that their life is a disappointment to their parents, and even to themselves.

It should be no surprise that adolescent depression, anxiety, and drug over-doses are at all-time highs, affecting even the most affluent American communities in epidemic proportions. Like it or not, all children are affected by the tentacles of a culture that is intolerant of failure in any form. The lessons from positive psychology unveiled in these stories are presented as an antidote to the current toxicity for teachers, parents, and, most importantly, students.

The simplicity of the strategy offered in this book is that powerful lessons on character strengths and developing a growth mindset are taught through the enchantment of picture books. The research on stories by Heath and Heath in *Made to Stick* found that interesting and creative stories have a neurological staying power deep within the brain.

Using picture books to shape student self-belief is built on a solid research foundation that enables students to paint a picture of the events in the story in a way that connects the story to the individual's personal life experience.
Each chapter book exploration has a specific positive psychology construct embedded within the story to help children grow a growth mindset and unlock their strengths. More importantly, each story has the power to create an episodic memory that can last a lifetime.

The essence of the latest positive psychology research is shared through these book-driven lessons in a way that transcends grade levels. The selected books and lessons that make up this edition have been used from pre-K to graduate school. Field tests with these lessons in college graduate school classes have found that adults can be as powerfully engrossed and mesmerized by the stories as younger children are. The response in the field tests has been overwhelmingly positive across all grade levels.

The hope is that this new application of children's literature serves as the impetus for important conversations that impart the roles of growth mindset, hope, grit, growth mindset, strengths, and happiness in individual journeys of everyone pursuing life goals and ambitions. The conversations that need to take place involve both students *and parents*. Although it is impossible to fully alter or reverse the current craziness and competitiveness of the culture, the goal is to introduce this research to help children to better cope with the demands of that culture.

Positive psychology research is radically and dramatically changing the landscape about the factors that lead to success and self-actualization. Shane Lopez of the Gallup Poll found that hope to be a better predictor of college completion than academic ability. Lopez's statistics reveal that students with low hope are four times more likely to not graduate college than students with low ability.

In research study after research study, what students believe about their future becomes their destiny. Duckworth's research and recent best seller clearly reveal that grit predicts success over ability in arena after arena. No such research linking increasing Common Core Standards to college completion or success in life exists. The ultimate reason educators need to incorporate this positive psychology innovation is that the stories and learning that follow may provide a clearer pathway to success for students than any other avenue available.

Chapter 2

The How

Lessons of Positive Psychology That You Can Teach Tomorrow

> With all that I have to do now, how will I ever find the time to deliver lessons in a content area that I am totally unfamiliar with and untrained in?

The lessons that follow provide a very detailed *how to* for teachers and schools to grow a growth mindset and to harness the character strengths of students. Underlying those lofty goals are two implicit beliefs. The first is that a growth mindset, the belief that learning is based on effort and not an inborn capacity, needs to be nurtured, developed, and *grown* in all students. The second is that every student, no matter what ability or current performance, has underlying strengths that need to be discovered and developed.

It is also the hope that these stories and ideas will make their way into the hands of parents, wise enough to employ the picture book literature in nightly reading in the absence of formal school curricula. A complete step-by-step methodology drives each chapter so that a parent can effectively explore these researched positive psychology understandings in enriching the nightly, bedtime read-aloud. Comprehensive lesson designs for educators are shared, but each of the lessons can be modified and the books can be used simply as a guided read-aloud.

The simplicity of stories that follow ensures that an advanced degree in psychology is not necessary. The magic of positive psychology is that it has the power to share much of the wisdom individuals have accrued about life, but lacked the research and terminology to support. The exciting part of the lesson activities is that, whatever the form of the lesson, there is almost a guarantee that the day's learning is shared over the dinner table that night.

This approach borrows heavily and with reverence from the *Philosophy for Kids* research and paradigm pioneered by Dr. Thomas Wartenberg of Mount Holyoke College. In fact, one might think about this text as *Positive*

Psychology for Kids. Dr: Wartenberg uses children's literature to share the ideas embraced in key schools of philosophy with even the youngest learners. In the *Philosophy for Kids* program, the lessons are truly learner-centered with students developing and constructing their own beliefs in regard to philosophy.

The design of this program differs slightly. The agenda of this book requires that students use picture books to discover snapshots of defined researched constructs and to internalize the language and understandings of positive psychology into their daily life experience. Each chapter lays out a framework for the questions needed to conduct a children's literature (picture book) discussion that leads beyond the Common Core listening objectives to analysis.

The positive psychology concepts in this book are the result of the extensive research by giants in the field, including Seligman (positive psychology); Dweck (growth mindset); Snyder and Lopez (hope); Duckworth (grit); Csikszentmihalyi (flow); Rath, Petersen, and Yeager (strengths); Frederickson (positivity); and Lyubomirsky (happiness). To make the psychology more user-friendly, the complex research that underlies each lesson is revealed in an abbreviated and simplified snapshot summary of the research findings at the start of each chapter.

More extensive resources and directions are provided on each psychological construct in the last chapter of the book. The psychology connections presented to begin each chapter should provide all that is needed in order to teach the children's book through a positive psychology lens.

However, teachers can enrich personal knowledge of the research by exploring the information provided in the last chapter to better inform their instruction. In other cases, teachers may use some of these same resources with children. When positive psychology takes hold, it does not easily let go. The authors are assured these references are only the beginning.

Each chapter begins with the C3 Inquiry Lesson Plan Template developed by the National Council of Social Studies. Each chapter's content is summarized on a one-page inquiry chart. This approach is now driving a new era of analysis and inquiry in the social studies.

The lessons are driven by a compelling question that requires a student to analyze evidence and, after investigation, develop a personal response to the question. This compelling question, made simple enough for the youngest child to understand, has been specifically designed to uncover the researched psychological foundation rooted in the story. The C3 Inquiry Template, standards, and rationale that define these lessons will be discussed in the next chapter in greater detail.

The specific children's literature selections that drive the book have been chosen to ensure that students make the connection between the big ideas of the book and their own personal experience. There are questions provided on the opening template to guide the teacher in the book discussion to link the events in the book with the child's life. The questions are suggestions for before the reading, during the reading, and after the reading.

It should also be clearly noted that the questions provided are merely starter questions and suggestions. It is in the intent and belief that discussion directions and questions are best left to each teacher. For this reason, the questioning spelled out in the template is not elaborated on in later text or extensively incorporated in the chapter discussion. There was a conscious attempt that the lesson design not resemble a module with specific questions that must be followed, but was purposely designed to be more open-ended for each teacher to plan.

The read-aloud discussions are followed up by homework that reinforces the relationship of the story and construct to the student's own life. Homework requires that students interact with parents or guardians through a reflective assignment that shares the learning and understanding of the lesson with the parent. This may end up being the most lasting and powerful focus of the book.

Those in education know that there is a need to educate parents on the lessons of positive psychology as much, or more than children. The chance of getting the majority of parents to an evening meeting to discuss positive psychology research and the secrets of self-belief might be slim to none. The curricular roadmap of each lesson involving parents through their child's homework may provide the ideal method of educating parents and guardians and powerfully sharing and reinforcing this learning.

Parental involvement serves as the backbone of the program. This vital component seeks not only to educate and involve the parents, but it also aspires to create an authentic community of sharing between parents, children, and the school. If teachers are to create a culture of grit, it cannot be built without educating and collaborating with informed parents.

The final aim in each chapter proposes that students translate learning to the real world. Students are required to take informed action offering avenues for the discovery and implementation of ways to share new positive psychology learning with others. This brings to life the mission of all social studies to create informed citizens with a civic desire to improve life on our planet for all.

These lessons on the constructs should not die in the classroom after completion, but the new learning should be applied to the real world in ways that will enable that learning to last long after the reading and lessons conclude. Only if this is able to be achieved will teachers, students, and parents be able to create environments that grow a growth mindset and unlock students' strengths.

Chapter 3

The Where

Curriculum Connections That Bring Common Core and NCSS C3 Standards to Life

> Where in the world can I integrate more into the curriculum, and how can I ever justify this to my administration?

Our goal is teaching these contents through children's literature to offer a solution to teachers, parents, and students for coping with the pressure of increasing and unyielding curricular expectations rather than adding to that burden. Real questions need to be first answered on *where* teachers can and should infuse these new content explorations into already—overstuffed days. The answer to that is a simple one.

Every lesson in this book is congruent with Common Core and National Social Studies Standards. Driving each lesson is the core belief and understanding that standards do matter and do need to drive student assignments and performances. The lessons that follow are not an attempt to sidestep the standards, but they provide a meaningful pathway to integrate those standards into the school day in ways that have the potential to redefine lives.

Using positive psychology to impart standards might actually provide the ideal methodology to put deep meaning and relevance into the standards. Positive psychology has the power to make the pursuit of standards feel less like a visit to the dentist's office. No disrespect to dentists is intended.

Standards, in their highest form, were not designed as lesson prescriptions, but were created to provide expectations and descriptors of excellence for students to strive for and aspire to. Standards are goals, not roadmaps. Examples of student writing as outcomes of our piloted lesson field tests have revealed that extraordinary and powerful writing connections have emerged from a curriculum that inspires students.

Teachers will find that language and vocabulary from the lesson activities will make their way into assignments long after the story and demonstrate

11

that the concepts and vocabulary have been internalized. Ironically, the lessons instill the dispositions and discipline that higher standards require and will help students better adjust to a culture of high expectations.

The goal is that the lessons that grow from these stories will arm teachers and parents with the necessary tools to instill in children a growth mindset *as a vehicle for imparting both Common Core and the new Social Studies Inquiry Standards.* Adjusting instruction to meet Common Core expectations need not be painful, but can become the best part of the day, if there is a passion for the writing and thinking required.

For those teachers or administrators with questions on the validity of the connections of the lessons to the standards, examining the following Common Core Anchor Standards should provide solid evidence that the lesson goals are truly standards based. You will find that as you review each lesson plan's standards and assignments on the templates that the expectations and requirements are in perfect synchrony with the proposed national standards.

COMMON CORE STANDARDS

Speaking and Listening Standards: Comprehension and Collaboration

1. Engage effectively in a range of collaborative discussions (one-on-one, in groups, and teacher-led) with diverse partners on topics and texts, building on others' ideas and expressing their own clearly.
   c. Pose and respond to specific questions by making comments that contribute to the discussion and elaborate on the remarks of others.
   d. Review the key ideas expressed and draw conclusions in light of information and knowledge gained from the discussions.
3. Ask and answer questions about what a speaker says in order to clarify comprehension, gather additional information, or deepen understanding of a topic or issue.

Writing Standards: Text Types and Purposes

1. Write opinion pieces on topics or texts, supporting a point of view with reasons and information.
   a. Introduce a topic or text clearly, state an opinion, and create an organizational structure in which ideas are logically grouped to support the writer's purpose.
   b. Provide logically ordered reasons that are supported by facts and details.

c. Link opinion and reasons using words, phrases, and clauses (e.g., consequently, specifically).

d. Provide a concluding statement or section related to the opinion presented.[3]

Perhaps, far more significantly, the lesson designs and questions are designed to build deep understanding that moves beyond the basic literacy skills of Common Core to impart the critical thinking skill of analysis. As students translate the deeper understanding in each story, the hope is that learners also develop metacognition about positive psychology and how it has shaped individual life experiences and beliefs.

In the analysis of children's literature stories, students are also required to reflect and build connections to analyze the personal unique characteristics that form their personality and the beliefs that have created that worldview. Hopefully, developing a deeper understanding of the character strengths behind success can facilitate a deeper student reflection and may influence and shape developing and evolving beliefs on life directions.

Although educators can all define and provide exemplars on what sound analysis looks like, few can offer practical ways to inspire analysis that offers challenges on a level that students can master. The summative requirements of the lesson require students to analyze each story thread, background knowledge, and sources to come to a personal conclusion on the compelling question.

Students must *analyze* evidence from the story and their lives as well as outside sources to frame an answer to the compelling question. This experience also provides a more secure platform for self-analysis as students can safely analyze the actions of a storybook character, rather than be forced to directly analyze more personal and intimate experiences that define the student's own life.

NATIONAL SOCIAL STUDIES THEMES AND STANDARDS

The curriculum that follows from the lessons powerfully incorporates the new NCSS Social Studies Toolkit template to ensure that the process of inquiry provides congruence in each psychological construct exploration. The C3 Framework is based on the understanding that there is more to a student's education than being college- or career-prepared.

The third C, C3, is that to be fully educated, students must be civically prepared to enter the world as functioning citizens. The ultimate purpose of social studies is to prepare students to function effectively in a democracy and diverse world. Discussions, activities, and connections surrounding the stories provide the ideal forum for the civic readiness that students need for effective citizenship.

The NCSS Themes and the NCSS Inquiry Arc

From New York State NCSS Toolkit Contributor April Francis

Although this book does not enter the realm of specific and direct social studies instruction with subject-specific text, it does powerfully address one of the major themes of the National Council for Social Studies (NCSS) ten strands of thematic instruction—Strand Four: Individual Development and Identity.

This theme often goes unnoticed as social studies seeks to arm students with the where, when, and why of the world. Though this theme has been largely overlooked in traditional social studies curricula, with the exception being high school psychology courses, positive psychology research is revealing that this omission at younger ages may be doing a great disservice to students.

Most social studies programs address each of the other nine themes powerfully and have local benchmarks, state assessments, and designed curricula to prove them, but little time or evidence can be found to delineating district's efforts or curricula on the theme of identity formation. Where in social studies programs can one find formal curricula on the tenets of the following Strand Four taken directly from the NCSS Handbook?

NATIONAL COUNCIL FOR SOCIAL STUDIES

Strand Four: Individual Development and Identity

- Questions related to identity and development, which are important in psychology, sociology, and anthropology, are central to the understanding of who we are. Such questions include: How do individuals grow and change physically, emotionally, and intellectually? Why do individuals behave as they do?
- The study of individual development and identity will help students to describe factors important to the development of personal identity. They will explore the influence of peoples, places, and environments on personal development. Students will hone personal skills such as demonstrating self-direction when working toward and accomplishing personal goals, and making an effort to understand others and their beliefs, feelings, and convictions.

Even though the NCSS College and Career and Civic Life (C3) Framework define effective social studies education that includes experiences that provide for the development of individual identity and development, few programs in the nation actually have documented designed formal curricula to meet this theme.

Many might contend that this theme is covered in the hidden curricula of a teacher's instruction and is integrated informally on a daily basis in the teachable moments and life lessons that come in dealing with developing children and social studies curricula. Reread the standards. Not only do the themes scream of the embedded positive psychology tenets embedded in children's literature presented here and in positive psychology research, but the content of these lessons seems far too important to leave to chance.

NATIONAL COUNCIL FOR SOCIAL STUDIES INQUIRY ARC

The lessons in this book attempt to utilize the C3 Framework to address *Strand Four: Individual Development and Identity* through the use of the Inquiry Arc. The Inquiry Arc, which is the foundation of the C3 Framework, requires educators to instill four dimensions within their curriculums: (1) developing questions and planning inquiries, (2) applying disciplinary concepts and tools, (3) evaluating sources and using evidence, and (4) communicating conclusions and taking informed action. It is the expectation that through these dimensions students are able to understand curriculum concepts through varied sources.

Once students acquire a base knowledge, they are encouraged to connect this knowledge to their everyday life and take action. Therefore, students are developing individuality and identity in civic ways. Yet, what is often overlooked in this approach is the understanding that for individuals to become civically involved, a platform to do so must be provided. This platform has been carefully designed by teachers to emerge from the lessons presented.

By employing an interdisciplinary version of the Inquiry Arc, incorporating literacy tools that reach the psychological and emotional strengths within our students, the curriculum is equipping children to develop their individuality and identity both civically and psychologically. The essential content called for by the NCSS is at the core of this work.

Standards Not Modules: New Curricular Approaches in an Age of Standards

The most appealing aspect of the Common Core literacy and Social Studies standards is that although the standards are clearly defined, the curricular directions to achieve the standards are designed to be open-ended. The most enlightened social studies and literacy programs have pursued high-level standards, but left the content choices in the hands of the teachers. This answers *the where* for the most creative and daring of educators. This is the opportunity to implement the lessons of positive psychology through children's literature.

The extremely enticing part of this proposed positive psychology explorations is that they need not be an "add-on" for overburdened teachers, but they can be used as the method to integrate the clearly defined Common Core and Social Studies goals for instruction in an engaging manner. The curriculum pathways in this program offer a creative way for teachers to meet the standards while engaging students and teaching life lessons.

The real objections to the Common Core lie not in the standards proposed, but in the dry, prescribed curricula or modules that are often aligned with a set of practices that do not inspire students or teachers. The remedy for those dry lessons is contained in the children's literature brought to life in each of the chapters that follow.

In employing these lessons to meet Common Core or Social Studies standards, teachers can be confident that each lesson builds in the psychological understanding that students need to handle the increasingly demanding challenges faced in this age of high-stakes assessments. Where this curriculum is injected into the school day and at to what degree is a decision left to each teacher, school system, or *parent at home.*

Charlotte Danielson in her article, *Teaching Like a Four Star Chef,* urges us to remember that Common Core Standards are not the meal we serve in a lesson, but merely the ingredients to a good meal. In almost the same way, the new inquiry direction in social studies suggests that the content of social studies is not merely information and details to be covered but is mastered to inform the learner in the process of analyzing information to make a sound decision.

With this in mind, it is the stories that make up a content that matter and the stories that follow connect, not only with positive psychology, but with the experiences that define a learner's life. These stories provide a content that has the potential and power to change the direction of a child's life. That seems to provide both a worthy meal and an important content topic for study.

Part II

CHILDREN'S LITERATURE LESSONS THAT TEACH GROWTH MINDSET AND UNLOCKING STUDENT STRENGTHS

Section II A: Growing a Growth Mindset: Learning to Fail Well

Chapter 4

Building a Growth Mindset
The Secret of Failing Well

The Girl Who Never Made Mistakes by Mark Pett and Gary Rubinstein

---

HOW THIS BOOK CONNECTS TO POSITIVE PSYCHOLOGY RESEARCH ON GROWTH MINDSET

The book *The Girl Who Never Made Mistakes* perfectly lays the foundation for helping students to understand the role of *failing well* at the heart of Carol Dweck's research on growth mindset by providing a humorous, but the powerful, example of a girl who fails well when all goes wrong in a community juggling performance. The book further shares the damaging weight that students might carry when trying to be perfect and live a life in fear of mistakes. The lesson plan that follows opens a window for students on the key tenets of positive psychology on which Dweck's theory of growth mindset is built.

Beatrice is introduced as a girl who never makes mistakes. At first, this seems to be an enviable trait in story. As the story goes on, the reader discovers that the pressure of being perfect and never failing does not seem to have Beatrice very happy. Students will discover this pressure to be perfect has left Beatrice somewhat disconnected and afraid to fail. The goal for students in answering the compelling questions on the template whether mistakes are good or bad arms students with a story that will stick that will forever define the concept of *failing well*.

Understanding that failure may often be only the first step in learning is at the heart of the research on growth mindset and is often referred to by positive psychologists as *failing well*. Carol Dweck in her book *Mindset: The New Psychology of Success* presents overwhelming research affirming the need for students to learn to view achievement as an incremental event based on effort rather than inborn capacity. The case is made that this *growth mindset* is essential if students are to achieve success in school and, ultimately, in life.

What follows here is a *snapshot* of the research and minimal groundwork needed to effectively connect Beatrice's story to the research, but be assured that materials, posters, worksheets, and ideas for teaching growth mindset abound and can be found instantaneously on Twitter or related social media on a daily *or hourly basis*. This introduction is not designed as a psychology text sharing the details of Dweck's research, but rather an overview that will enable you to link the big ideas of the existing research to the story.

A growth mindset is a view of learning as a process that is driven by effort that involves constant growth through trial and error. It is a mindset that believes that failure may be a necessary building block for success and failing can teach children the lessons that can often be learned in no other way. Students, with a growth mindset, view failures as signal that more effort is needed, rather than a measure that innate ability or capacity is lacking.

Growth mindset enables students, and their parents, to see the increasing complexity of school as a challenge and to handle increasing errors as part of the process of learning, rather than a judgment on innate talent abilities. As opposed to growth mindset, the fixed mindset views learning as a measure of the capacity or innate abilities of the learner.

Fixed mindset implies exactly what the word suggests: *ability has a fixed capacity or ceiling*. On first meeting, the reader is led to believe Beatrice's talents are inborn and immutable. Beatrice appears infallible and is celebrated by all for this talent of never making a mistake. As the story goes on, the reader discovers that Beatrice is prisoner of a fixed mindset belief.

The suggestion at the heart of this book is that Beatrice has been blessed with this innate ability from birth. Ironically, Beatrice's brother has not been blessed with such a talent and lives a life unafraid of convention or mistakes, but seems wildly happier than Beatrice.

Beatrice is also portrayed as doing all things without effort. In fact, if great effort is needed, fixed mindsets might view this effort as an indictment of the capacity of the individual. When students are heard to say that he or she does well in school, *but that person studies a lot*, the *study a lot* part is not meant to be viewed as a compliment, but is seen as proof that the individual is not all that smart. The implication is that if students need to study a lot, the student is lacking in innate and natural talent.

This *fixed mindset* can view failure as a condemnation of the overall intelligence or ability. When students do exceptionally well early in life, parents, or teachers and coaches often beam with pride at early success and proclaim that these children are *naturals* as scholars, athletes, geniuses, or artists. What is implied is that these capacities are inborn. Beatrice is certainly a natural.

Failure is an assault on these labels and can be viewed with hostility by both children and parents. This mindset can result in children shying away from greater challenges that might threaten perceived capacity and being jealous of the success of other children, as threatening to assumed capacities. In the story, Beatrice shies away from ice-skating because it is fraught with challenge and potential failure.

Dweck's research indicates that as school becomes more complex and challenging, fixed mindset students tend to plateau and peak, while growth mindset children continue to grow and achieve at higher levels of complexity. Dweck's research about the plateauing effect of a fixed mindset holds for every level, even advanced graduate school levels, including medical school.

Positive psychologists have labeled this ability to view failure as a stepping-stone to success as *failing well* and defined it with specific traits. Firstly, failing well is learning from mistakes so that an individual can learn what not to do on the way to learning what to do. Of course, failing badly in the extreme is not learning from mistakes and making the same mistake again and again. Failing badly ultimately results in quitting altogether.

What is needed if you are to fail well is a mindset in which the learner accepts responsibility for the mistake rather than blames other individuals. Blame can be placed in many directions, including other individuals, including the teacher, the coach, parents, or the situation conditions. Some students might even blame the test or how the individual was feeling on that day. Failing badly involves making excuses and blaming others or sometimes even the conditions. *The room was too noisy, how could I concentrate on the test?*

Finally, if failure is to result in flourishing, the student must not embrace a negative worldview on failure itself. If students view failure through a fixed mindset lens, as a condemnation of their innate ability, there is little likelihood that they will accept responsibility and learn from the mistake. If students view failure as pervasive, something that will always happen, they will only view future failures as further proof of a lack of ability or capacity.

What is needed if one is to *fail well* is a view on failure, not as an indictment of ability, but as an opportunity for growth and learning. Despite the temporary pain involved in failure, students must learn to view setbacks as potentially positive experiences. Without this positive attitude as a foundation, there is little likelihood that children will fail well.

The conclusion of the story offers a template for students to analyze Beatrice's failure and enables students to decide on their own about Beatrice's reaction to failure. The hope is that the book is a springboard for students to analyze personal reactions to failure.

More detailed information on growth mindset research is available for the teacher or the parent in the reference section in Chapter 20 of this book. These shared sources on growth mindset include YouTube presentations, life-altering books applying the research to daily life, and a snapshot of the scholarly research from which the positive psychology supporting the chapter has been derived. Teachers are encouraged to dig deeper into developing a rich understanding of the research in order to strengthen the power and delivery of the lesson.

Lesson Design: *The Girl Who Never Made Mistakes*
Kevin Sheehan

Table 4.1.　The Secret of Failing Well: *The Girl Who Never Made Mistakes*

Compelling Question	Are mistakes good or bad?	
Common Core Standards	• CCSS.ELA-LITERACY.CCRA.R.2 • CCSS.ELA-LITERACY.CCRA.SL.1 • CCSS.ELA-LITERACY.CCRA.W.1 • NCSS—Theme 4: Individual Development and Identity • NCSS Inquiry Arc—Dimension 4	
Staging the Question	• Discuss whether mistakes are good or bad. • Watch the video and discuss why the girl is afraid to answer a math question in class.	

Supporting Question 1 (Before reading) What are your feelings about mistakes?	Supporting Question 2 (During reading) How did Beatrice fail well in The Girl Who Never Made Mistakes?	Supporting Question 3 (After reading) How can we fail well in our lives?
Are mistakes good or bad? What was it like when you first learned to ride a bike, write your name, or do long division? Why was the student in the YouTube video afraid to answer the math question? Are you ever afraid to answer a question in class? Are mistakes good or bad?	Why does Beatrice have reporters outside her door? Who seems happier, Beatrice or her brother? Where did Beatrice get the idea that she should not make mistakes? Why does Beatrice not skate with her friends? Why is Beatrice nervous after her almost mistake? Is she happy?	Did Beatrice fail well? How would she feel if she had failed badly? Was Beatrice happier as the girl who made mistakes or the girl who never made mistakes? How do you know? Did you ever feel like her in any way? Do you know anyone like her?

Formative Performance Task	Formative Performance Task	Formative Performance Task
The teacher presents students with questions to elicit where students are in regard to their views on failure. Students will view a video on a student afraid to answer a question in class.	Students respond to the above questions at key points in the text.	Students will sort the qualities of failing well from the diagram as presented in the lesson text in a format chosen by the teacher. The teacher will create a mystery for students to sort their failing well choices from failing badly choices.
Featured Sources	**Featured Sources**	**Featured Sources**
Afraid to Answer in Math Class YouTube Video https://www.youtube.com/watch?v=UNAMrZr9OWY	*The Girl Who Never Made Mistakes* By Mark Pett and Gary Rubinstein	Materials—Teacher Created Mystery

Summative Performance Task	**Argument**	Students will answer the compelling question in a Common Core opinion essay.
	Extension	Students will retell the story to their parents and elicit a time their parents failed well. Students will draw a picture or share a story of their parents failing well with the class.
Taking Informed Action (Enrichment)		Students will share the story of their parents failing well and will create a school bulletin board or a Twitter handle to inform the community.

STAGING THE LESSON

There are a great many YouTube videos on failing well that can be easily obtained from a Google search to set the stage for the book that follows. One of the best ways to set the stage for this lesson involves a 55-second clip by *GoStrengths online* on fixed versus growth mindsets in children (https://www.youtube.com/watch?v=UNAMrZr9OWY). *GoStrengths* produces a host of extraordinary teaching videos that can be purchased online.

This clip depicts the story of a young girl in class who is afraid to answer because the answer might be wrong. This clip provides a perfect takeoff for the book and the idea of a fixed mindset. After the video, it will be easy to elicit responses on why the girl will not answer a simple math question, while the friend gives it a shot. This clip sets up clear pathways to the idea of growth mindset, introducing the big idea at the heart of the book.

With this simple starter, the teacher can begin simply enough with the compelling question as the starting point. *Are mistakes good or bad?* This simple question can be understood at the kindergarten level and equally wrestled with by graduate students. The key to your questioning is to build on each answer by posing the opposite point of view in a follow-up question that stretches student understanding.

If the majority of students present the sophisticated view that mistakes are natural and healthy, students can be easily stretched to see the opposite point of view by suggesting to themselves that one might want to make a lot of mistakes on the next test or the admission to college testing. Students will immediately understand that the question is more complex than it seems and opens them to a new mindset.

With directed questioning by the teacher, students tend to eventually move toward the view that mistakes can lead to greater success if responded to in the right way. The opening discussion should be a chance for the teacher to take the pulse of the class on the question and set the stage for the book.

Younger children generally tend to overwhelmingly support the hypothesis that mistakes are inherently bad. Older students will be more conflicted by the question knowing that they are politically supposed to answer that mistakes are good, but having been scarred by the idea that mistakes are painful and often barriers to entry in life. This opening discussion should cause some dissonance in students as they begin to be less certain about views. The discussion should introduce the idea that more thought should be given to how we view mistakes.

On the early elementary level, the discussion should begin with reminding questions about failures that ended in positive outcomes that they are already familiar with. Questions might ask students to recall the experience of riding a bike or writing one's name for the first time. Strangely enough, most kindergarteners seem to recall positive experiences in learning to ride a bike, forgetting the bumps, bruises, and falls. Nearly all kindergarten students will recall recent trauma of writing one's name and testify that this process involves a good amount of trial and a great deal of painful *error*.

In any grade level, the opening questioning should involve a framing that seeks out experiences where the students experienced failure on the way to success. Older students can often provide failures that taught life lessons with more elaborate recall and stories.

With this brief mental framing in place, children are ready and excited for the read-aloud to begin. The lead-in to introduce the book might be presented to students suggesting that this is a story, unlike the girl afraid to be wrong in the YouTube clip, about a girl who is never wrong. *This book is about a girl who never made mistakes.*

THE READ-ALOUD: STORIES THAT STICK

Questions before, during, and after the reading are on the template and are provided merely as suggestions. It is the belief of the authors that questions used to drive the reading are best created by the individual classroom teacher as part of the teachable moments that make read-aloud experiences come to life. The suggestions on the template might be used to get the lesson started, and follow-up questions should naturally arise in response to students' reactions.

Summative Performance Tasks

In order to follow up on the lesson, it is important to have students move from the story to the theories behind the story. There are as many different approaches to achieving this goal as there are teaching techniques. Teachers have to make their own gravy in education and choose the ingredients and approach that best satisfy individual style and preference.

Immediately after story students might be presented with the research tenets below to review the story. The approaches can vary from making large oak tag posters on the concepts below as class discussion pieces, using smart board technology to display the concepts or having students work in pairs to solve the teacher mystery of *failing well*. In each case, students should take from the lesson through large class discussion, group work, or individual reflection the keys to *failing well* listed here.

Whatever approach is chosen, students should conclude the read-aloud by correctly connecting the building blocks of *Failing Well* and *Failing Badly* (Table 4.2) with Beatrice's actions in the story and ultimately their own lives.

One way to do this is to create a mystery. This template can be called a mystery and cutup and placed in an envelope with teams of students discussing and then placing the cutup sheets of paper under the appropriate headings as a paired or individual activity. In the teacher resources section, there is a simplified example of the situations that students will sort under the headings *Failing Well* or *Failing Badly*.

In other cases, teachers might employ technology to create the same level and type of sorting challenge activity. Whatever methodology is employed, students should be able to identify and correctly sort the key elements of *Failing Well* and *Failing Badly* at the end of the read-aloud and follow-up. The activity should leave students to ready to answer the compelling question with concrete evidence.

Table 4.2. Failing Well, Failing Badly Chart

Failing Well	Failing Badly
Taking Responsibility for Failure: Blaming No One	Blaming Others or Circumstances: Not Taking Responsibility for Failure
Learning Valuable Lessons from Failure	Not Learning Valuable Lessons from Failure: Repeating the Same Mistake Over and Over
Having a Positive Attitude on Failure (Growth Mindset)	Having a Negative Attitude on Failure (Fixed Mindset)

Extension

The real power of this lesson is that this extension activity is essential and involves a requirement that the lesson goes home and is shared with parents. There are numerous ways to share the story at home. One of the easiest ways is to have students and parents or guardians Google the trailer for the book on the Internet, but a more powerful way is to have students or the class as a whole identify five key phrases and retell parents the story at home.

The written part of the homework assignment is for students to then ask their parents to relate a story about a time when *they failed well* and grew from failure. After hearing the story, students are then to draw a picture of the *failed well* experience. (Instructions may need to be provided for parents on the concept of *failing well*.)

These pictures can be shared the next day as each student reinforces the concept by sharing these stories. The power of stories is that there is good deal of brain research that tells this learning will be more permanent as the brain will record the story as it were a movie, employing different areas of the brain to store the information.

Older students may wish to use Twitter or video to create their own Twitter handle (#teachers name failing well stories) with collected as video posts of their parents' stories made from phones. Another strategy might be to use Tellagami or any application that allows the parents' stories to be shared through an animated character.

There is no limit to how this lesson can be shared at home with parents and made real and permanent to students. What is essential and under the radar is that parents are being educated alongside their children. These positive psychology building blocks that are forming a foundation in children are now also being cemented in the minds and hearts of parents.

Argument

In our age of Common Core accountability, it is necessary to have students consolidate their understanding of these concerns by answering the compelling question in writing. These writing pieces should be driven by the same standards and rubrics as all Common Core opinion-writing assignments (see Standards).

Emphasis should be placed on asking students to bring forth evidence from the story, individual life experiences, and the surrounding world to make an argument to answer the compelling question, *Are mistakes good or bad?* Students should be encouraged to incorporate the tenets of *failing well* as part of their evidence or thesis. Arguments should be more than just how a student feels about the question but should include real-world evidence to make a case.

Taking Informed Action

Perhaps the best way to make this learning permanent in children is to require that they take an action that brings learning to a real-world audience. Again the ways to do this are as numerous as there are stories of *failing well*, but a great place to begin is to ask students how they can keep alive and share the idea of *failing well* with classes that come after them or with other classes in the school.

This might involve students creating a school bulletin board in which students (*and parents*) maintain an ongoing bulletin display that celebrates failures that involve learning valuable lessons and growing from those lessons. Students might post this bulletin board outside the classrooms as an up-to-the-minute living museum that keeps alive the understandings gleaned from this read-aloud.

Older students might create a Twitter handle or a Facebook page that shares these stories with the outside world. Still other efforts could seek to write a letter to incoming students in the next year about the idea of *failing well* that drives the class mindset. Finally, more creative students might want to create their own picture books on *failing well*.

In whatever way that the class decides to share these insights, the research is clear on the fact that the learning will be made more permanent by the students teaching these lessons to others and that the efforts that arise from producing work for a real-world audience will be far greater than any efforts that the students will put forth for a grade.

Teacher Resources

Figure 4.1.   Figure Failing Well, Failing Mystery Sheet

Table 4.3. Failing Well Mystery Examples

The test was unfair! My teacher did not prepare us for that test.	The test was fair. I should not have gone to the party before the test.
I will do better next time.	I just cannot do math! My mother could not do it either!
The teacher hates me.	I did not do well; I guess I am going to have to work a lot harder.
I am going to have to put way more effort into this work.	This is too hard. I am quitting.

These situations can be created by the teacher to embrace any of the criteria that define failing well and failing badly. Once created, these situations are cut into slips of paper, placed in an envelope so that students can then collaboratively as a team sort them on the following chart as examples of failing well or failing badly.

Failing Well	Failing Badly

Figure 4.2. Failing Well Answer Sheet

Chapter 5

Foundation for a Fixed Mindset

The Dangers of Naturals

Noel the First by Kate McMullen

HOW THIS BOOK CONNECTS TO POSITIVE PSYCHOLOGY RESEARCH ON GROWTH MINDSET

Noel the First dramatically portrays the idea of a *natural*, revealing the extent to which students may go to convince others that talent or ability is inborn and natural. The story translates Carol Dweck's mindset research on the dangers that can arise when children are praised for innate talent rather than effort to a story that every child can identify with.

Although this story is about ballet, the dangers of believing that some of us have "it" and others don't extend to every area of life from academics to athletics. The real damage of this mindset can be seen not only in its effect on the students trying to live up to the label *natural*, but on the students who believe that they are not naturals. For these students, effort comes to be viewed as futile.

When students do exceptionally well early in life, parents, or teachers and coaches, often beam with pride at early success and anoint these children as *naturals* as scholars, athletes, geniuses, or artists. What is implied is that these capacities are inborn. Failure can be viewed as an assault on the idea that students are naturally talented and can be viewed with hostility by both children and their parents.

This mindset can result in children shying away from greater challenges that might threaten this heightened sense of capacity, being jealous of the success of other children, viewing that the success of others is threatening to their assumed capacities. In *Noel the First*, all of these dangers come to life through the story.

Parents may sometimes enthusiastically embrace this idea of natural talent as a reflection of genetically passed-down talents or abilities. The danger of embedding the idea that talent is an attribute may result in increasing the worst possible symptoms of the fixed mindset. Individuals who are labeled as *naturals* can often only prove that they are not always naturals when faced with more demanding challenges. Teachers and parents are often the worst culprits celebrating the success of children as prodigies rather than recognizing the effort behind all success.

As a result of celebrity, *naturals* often avoid more demanding tasks or more rigorous teachers, as a lack of success may be an indicator that the praise showered on them as naturals is unwarranted. Students who have been labeled as a "natural" may also view the success of fellow students as a threat to their capacity and react with jealousy. Rather than be stimulated and inspired by the success of classmates as those with a growth mindset are, students who feel that talent is natural may see fellow students' success as a threat to their natural ability.

Finally, the worst outcome may be that those labeled as naturals may associate coaching or constructive criticism with frustration and resistance. Since their talent is natural, the idea of direction from an adult or peer may disconfirm the underlying belief that talent is natural. Those with a growth mindset understand that coaching and direction are essential to their success.

Noel the First realistically portrays the appeal of being thought of as naturally talented and the draining effects that this mindset can have on performance and well-being. Noel first begins to think of herself as *Noel the First* when awarded the first spot on the balance beam in ballet class. This belief and confidence is soon eroded as a newcomer to class, Anne Marie, dazzles the class with a truly awe-inspiring ballet performance.

When asked about her previous history in ballet, Anne Marie lies and says that this is her first time doing ballet. When Anne Marie is given the first spot on the bar, Noel is no longer able to perform the ballet moves that she once did so gracefully without thinking. Noel is no longer the natural, and her confidence and ability erode. All of this starts to change when Noel discovers Ann Marie's leotard is made of velvet and was the same one that students had worn in ballet classes in earlier years when beginning ballet lessons.

Anne Marie confesses to have taken ballet since she was two and admits to lying about it when she began. All of the realities of wanting others to believe that you have natural talent and not talent borne of effort come crashing through at this point in the story. The plot thickens as a new natural, Regina Louisa Belinda, takes the first spot and Noel is moved to third on the beam.

When the class is going to perform *Cinderella*, Anne Marie and Regina Louisa Belinda, seeking only to be number one on bar, are terrible in their dance. At this point, Noel forgets about being number one, the natural, and remembers how much she loves to dance as she turns into Cinderella before the class's eyes. Her performance ignores who is number one, and her effort and passion for dancing come shining through in her performance.

This book imparts lessons to teachers, parents, and coaches on the danger of labeling and anointing children who demonstrate early proficiency. The dangers are as great for those labeled first on the beam as for others not first on the beam. This book needs to be read by all teachers in regard to the dangers of praising children for natural ability. Parents and teachers must learn to praise effort and not capacity.

More detailed information on growth mindset research is available for the teacher or the parent in the reference section in Chapter 20 of this book. These shared sources on growth mindset include YouTube presentations, life-altering books applying the research to daily life, and a snapshot of the scholarly research from which the positive psychology supporting the chapter has been derived. Teachers are encouraged to dig deeper into developing a rich understanding of the research in order to strengthen the power and delivery of the lesson.

Lesson Design: *Noel the First*
Kathleen Neagle Sokolowski

Table 5.1. The Dangers of Naturals: *Noel the First* by Kate McMullen

	Noel the First
Compelling Question	Is there a danger in being labeled "a natural"?
Common Core Standards	• CCSS.ELA-LITERACY.CCRA.R.2 • CCSS.ELA-LITERACY.CCRA.SL.1 • CCSS.ELA-LITERACY.CCRA.W.1 • NCSS—Theme 4: Individual Development and Identity • NCSS Inquiry Arc—Dimension 4
Staging the Question	Students participate in the SMART Strengths I and E School of Turning Simulation.

Supporting Question 1	*Supporting Question 2*	*Supporting Question 3*
(Before reading) What is a natural? *Where does one* labeled a natural *get one's* talent from?	*(During reading) What* happens to Noel when her innate talent is threatened in ballet class in Noel the First?	*(After reading) What are* the potential problems of those labeled a natural for those not labeled naturals?

Continued

Table 5.1. Continued

Have you ever been in a situation where someone is just a natural? In sports, in arts, in music, in academics, how do "naturals" make you feel? Is there a danger to being a natural?	Why does Ann Marie lie about never doing ballet before? How did Madam treat Noel when she was first? How did she treat her when she was third? Do teachers and coaches create the idea of first and second? What has Noel learned from no longer being first?	Why does Noel dance the way she does? Why do Ann Marie and Regina Louisa Belinda dance the way they do? What is a lesson we can all learn from *Noel the First*?
Formative Performance Task	*Formative Performance Task*	*Formative Performance Task*
The students are questioned to elicit where they are in regard to their views on being a natural. Students will write their initial ideas on what it's like to be "naturally good" (or not) at something.	Students turn and talk to a partner to discuss the previous questions at key points in the text.	Students will exchange their initial writing with another student in the class. Students will write back to each other, letter style, to share new feelings and ideas on the idea of being a natural.
Featured Sources	*Featured Sources*	*Featured Sources*
	Noel the First by Kate McMullan	"Courage of Famous Failures" https://www.youtube.com/watch?v=Ydeyl0vXdP0

Summative Performance Task	**Argument**	Students will identify areas where they may be a "natural" and areas where skills do not come as easily through a discussion on the Marble Theory of Intelligence. Students will think of a person they admire and write a letter to him or her. In the letter, students will ask if the person considers himself or herself to be a "natural" or someone who worked hard to become a success.
	Extension	Students will retell the story to their families and interview a family member about his or her experiences with natural skills versus effort. Students can watch the video https://www.youtube.com/watch?v=Ydeyl0vXdP0.
Taking Informed Action (Enrichment)		Students can create a display with the words "Natural" on one side and "Effort" on the other. As they receive responses from the people they wrote to, pictures of the people could be placed near the word that most describes how they became successful.

STAGING THE LESSON

This staging activity has been borrowed with deep respect and gratitude from the SMART Strengths research and text developed by John Yeager, Sherri Fischer, and David Shearon. More information can be found on their research in the bibliography and sections on strengths.

To begin this lesson, the teacher announces the class will take part in a School of Turning! The class is randomly divided in half. The first group of students will be in the "E School of Turning." The teacher will quickly and simply show these children how to spin around, and then ask them to spin once. After the spin, one student will be singled out as a magnificent spinner and turner, and the teacher will lavish praise on the child and ask the child to demonstrate how it should be done for the class.

The other students will be largely ignored as the one "natural" is complimented for spinning prowess. The more that the teacher can gush about the performance, the more effective will be the power of praise and the feeling that the rest of the class has toward the "natural." Each time the rest of the students spin, the activity will be halted and the class will be directed to watch and learn from the one singled-out "natural."

Next, the other students in the "I School of Turning" will have a turn. This time, the teacher will coach all participants with attention to specific detail on how to turn in the most effective manner and the teacher will offer encouraging words to the whole group about their effort. The teacher will praise the effort of each turner, regardless of ability.

The teacher will teach each group again to increase the power of the simulation. In the "E" group, some of the students will be labeled as "Ls" and some as "almost Ls," but not told what these terms mean. On their own, students will begin to surmise from the teacher's attitude that "L" means loser.

After the second group sits down, the teacher will open up the conversation about what students noticed about the differences between groups. The teacher will ask how the first group, in the "E School of Turning," felt, including the student who was singled out apart from the others. The teacher will determine if the students in the "L" grouping had any inkling of what "L" stood for. In every simulation to date, students have garnered the meaning of the term.

Next, the teacher will ask the students in the "I School of Turning" about their experience and how it felt as they spun around. The teacher will elicit from students how the teacher's teaching practice was different for each group. Students will almost always automatically connect and share their own "I" and "E" School experiences.

The teacher will elicit from the students how it feels to be a natural at something and receive a lot of compliments about their ability, and how it feels to not be that student. The teacher will draw out the differences between being praised for their effort as opposed to being coached and complimented for their effort.

The teacher will reveal that the "E" stood for "entity," which basically means an individual either has the skill or doesn't. The "I" represented "incremental" growth, meaning an individual could get better in increments, through practice and effort. The class will discuss why the natural spinner might start to worry if the compliments about the individual's spinning talent stop or are directed at others. Being praised for being naturally good at something will begin to unravel as having potential drawbacks.

The students will take some time to write about their ideas of what it means to be a natural at something. Do they consider themselves a natural at anything? Have they been around other kids who are praised for being naturals? Would you take chances and try new things if you worried about disappointing someone who praised you often?

THE READ-ALOUD: STORIES THAT STICK

The students are now ready to engage in the read-aloud exploring the story in whatever format that the teacher shares to read the story. Questions before, during, and after the reading are on the template and are provided merely as suggestions.

It is the belief of the authors that questions used to drive the reading are best created by the individual classroom teacher as part of the teachable moments that make read-aloud experiences come to life. More than likely, the suggestions will get you started and follow-up questions will arise in response to students' reactions.

SUMMATIVE PERFORMANCE TASKS

Summing up the lesson will teach students to realistically understand that individuals do have certain areas of strength and interest where accomplishment might result more easily and "naturally." Although these areas might make individuals view this talent as "natural," students will learn that only great effort will cultivate and develop these talents or interest. In addition, students will learn that many areas will not come naturally and that these areas will require more effort to develop.

In exploring this concept of the "natural," have students think about their individual strengths and interests as areas that involve struggle and frustration. In *Learn Like a Pirate* (2015), Paul Solarz describes the Marble Theory. This theory serves to "level the playing field" and to help students to realize that all individuals have unique talents, gifts, and interests.

The Marble Theory states that people are all born with the same number of marbles in their brains. When individuals are born, these marbles are just in a big pile, but over time, individuals allocate these marbles into cups that represent unique skills, talents, interests, and abilities. Individuals can have as many cups as needed, and these cups are extremely specialized.

For example, there is not a single cup for reading abilities. Instead, several cups for reading might exist: one dedicated to decoding, one for literal comprehension, one for inferential comprehension, one for reading fluency, and so on. But people might also have cups dedicated to dribbling a basketball, drawing horses, telling jokes, playing the flute, and so on. The theory suggests that individuals are all equal in terms of intelligence and ability.

Underlying the theory is the belief that intelligence needs to be measured differently. Due to grades and report cards, students learn to think of themselves as smart or dumb. Low grades do little more than disappoint and discourage students. High grades can often create perfectionists and cause children to become extrinsically motivated.

The teacher might first gather students in a circle, with a jar full of marbles and small cups nearby. Explaining the Marble Theory, the teacher will share with the students as to how the teacher would distribute talents in labeled cups, describing a personal perception of abilities, talents, and interests. If the teacher feels very confident about the ability to teach reading, that cup would have more marbles, then, say, the cooking cup. It is important to share with students that the level of marbles is not fixed. If the teacher took cooking lessons or spent more time learning about cooking, more marbles could be added.

After the demonstration, students will make their own cups enumerating personal strengths and divide a prescribed, but equal, number of distributed marbles. This activity can be done with the actual cups and marbles, or through sketching, or a digital representation.

Students might also write and create a video of describing the cups their individual cups and reasoning behind the level of marbles in each cup. Apps such as *SeeSaw* allow students to put pictures and video in a digital portfolio that is shared with the parents. As the year progresses, students could reflect upon any changes made by strengthening areas of weakness, thus adding more marbles to that cup.

TAKING INFORMED ACTION

Now that the students have identified areas where individual talent might seem "natural" and areas that they feel less confident, the teacher could pose the question about successful people in our world that we might be tempted to consider as naturals. Were these individuals "naturals" and always excellent in chosen fields or was their talent borne of effort? Students will now watch the video to see how people we think of as legends actually failed quite a bit before finding success: https://www.youtube.com/watch?v=Ydeyl0vXdP0.

With the idea in mind that our legends often were not naturals, students will identify people personally admired. The person could be "famous" or someone they know. Would those people say that having natural talent was more important than putting forth great effort? Students could compose letters to their heroes, asking that question.

Letters might be linked and tweeted to the person, mailed, or hand-delivered. As students receive responses, the class will keep track of the responses that favor natural talent and the responses that share that effort made the difference.

Another interesting question to have students ask might be if the person always loved what he or she does. Is it important to be the best at something or to enjoy doing it? Connecting back to *Noel the First*, Noel was happiest when she danced with her heart and didn't worry about being the first at the bar. These questions lay the foundation for chapters that will follow.

While there is much to teach the students in this lesson, there is also much for the teacher to keep in mind about the language they use to encourage students as teachers. Are we unwittingly acting as Madam and ranking students by our words, gestures, or expressions? Does our commentary encourage everyone and praise effort and progress?

Do teachers unknowingly communicate to some that the idea that a student's accomplishment is the product of natural talent or ability? Should teachers consider the dangers in labeling students? How can teachers better communicate and celebrate the unique talents, strengths, and hard work that make each child shine?

Chapter 6

Threats to a Growth Mindset

The Peril of Performance Goals

Book: *Too Perfect* by Trudy Ludwig

HOW THIS BOOK CONNECTS TO POSITIVE PSYCHOLOGY RESEARCH ON GROWTH MINDSET

Too Perfect offers students a firsthand look at the dangers that result when students seek perfection in *performance* goals. A performance goal centers on the evaluation of how close an individual comes to attaining a desired performance rating, result, or score on a task. A mastery goal involves mastering the knowledge, skills, and dispositions of the task, in effect mastering the skill that underlies the task. In simplest terms, a performance goal can often be reduced to getting a 100 on a test and/or achieving the score or result, in short winning the game.

The drive to be the best in our now-globally competitive culture has made performance goals measured by test scores and athletic victories more sought after than ever. Students today often end up measuring themselves against a defined score, not by the mastery of a curriculum or skill, but by the evaluation that they receive on performance. Even after a youth sports contest, the first and most common question heard is, "Did you win?"

Performance goals can often be the measuring sticks of success and can often be the rewards that help nurture a fixed mindset belief system. In this system, a single score can validate or invalidate one's ability and worth. A performance goal is a goal that strives for a specific grade on a test, sales quota, or a winning score in a game. If an individual achieves the performance goal, no matter how much is learned or actually mastered in pursuit of that goal, he or she has successfully met the desired outcomes. After achieving a performance goal, an individual's motivation and interest in a topic often dissipates as the desired performance has been achieved.

Mastery goals are goals in which you seek to master the specific area of study or a skill, with less emphasis on getting a good score and more on mastering the essence of the task. Goals that reflect mastery as always beyond one's reach can never be totally fully attained. Mastery goals demand that individuals persevere and maintain long-term motivation beyond the performance in pursuit of mastery.

When students adopt performance goals, there is a danger of embracing the negative characteristics that define fixed mindset beliefs. Motivated only by extrinsic measures, students are tempted to avoid more challenging tasks or demanding teachers in hopes of scoring higher or performing well on easier tasks. These students may also view fellow students as competition and develop resentment toward successful classmates.

Perhaps the worst outcome of performance goals is the performance anxiety that arises from the desire to achieve only external rewards. Research has revealed that the anxiety to achieve external rewards can actually inhibit performance and derail mastery of a topic or skill (learning).

Many parents have lived through the nightmare of a child trying to pass a road test (performance) rather than demonstrating *mastery* of driving skill. On the second road test, the child is often able to break down the anxious, emotional control of the brain and the resulting anxiety to perform that makes performance impossible. The same shift from paralysis over anxiety over performance to a focus on mastery of content is needed if those struggling with the anxiety of achieving a passing score on a test are to eventually meet success.

Too Perfect is a story that shockingly reveals the dangers and potential damage of performance goals. On our first meeting, Maisie is unhappy with her levels of measured performance in academics, ability in athletics, and even personal appearance. Despite mother's admonition that *she is perfect just the way she is*, life is giving scores and evaluations that make it difficult to accept mother's appraisal.

When Maisie encounters Kayla, it becomes even harder to accept her mother's beliefs, as Kayla seems to be everything that Maisie longs to be in the classroom, on the athletic field, and in appearance. The story gradually reveals the damaging effect that seeking to perfect as measured by performance goals has had on Kayla. Maisie eventually comes to appreciate that there is a danger in striving to be perfect in measured performance goals. The story reveals that "being perfect" is not only not always an attainable goal, but also it may become a destructive goal.

This is the final selection in the mindset literature, because today children's success is more than ever measured by performance indicators and scores.

Although students may adopt the belief and values of a growth mindset, there is a pervasive evaluation of performance measured in comparison to others. Any doubt about this axiom can be dispelled by checking your district's communication on where your child stacks up in math, language arts, or even physical conditioning in relation to students in your school, region, state, and the nation.

Too Perfect needs to be shared and understood by both parents and students to avoid the perils that befall Kayla in her obsession to be perfect on performance measures alone. An essential part of a growth mindset is the idea to encourage students to have patience with measured performance as they grow. The idea that "Maisie is a perfect Maisie" is one that she can understand only after witnessing the demise of her talented friend in pursuit of perfection.

Alfie Kohn in his groundbreaking work, *Punished by Rewards*, attacked the damage done by our school systems to students driven by rewards that range from grades to gold stars. His premise that the pursuit of these rewards issued for performance goals results in negative outcomes for the students judged on numbers rather than on learning.

At the heart of growth mindset, the focus on mastery goals most supports Kohn's basic beliefs that students are punished by extrinsic rewards and truly driven by intrinsic rewards. *Too Perfect* makes Kohn's case dramatically and offers to teachers and parents a plea for common sense and patience in pursuit of the performance goals as the current standard for measuring success in our schools.

The need to implant the idea of learning as seeking mastery rather than performance underlies this story and is essential if educators are to complete the foundation for growing a growth mindset. Students need to be aware that they are not the test scores that they receive. *Too Perfect* can open that discussion and plant a picture in the memory of students on the danger of not realizing that they are far more than any score can measure.

More detailed information on growth mindset research is available for the teacher or the parent in the reference section in Chapter 20 of this book. These shared sources on growth mindset include YouTube presentations, life-altering books applying the research to daily life, and a snapshot of the scholarly research from which the positive psychology supporting the chapter has been derived. Teachers are encouraged to dig deeper into developing a rich understanding of the research in order to strengthen the power and delivery of the lesson.

Lesson Design: *Too Perfect*
Kathleen Nicoletti-Blake and Anthony J. Marino

Table 6.1. The Perlin of Performance Goals: *Too Perfect* by Trudy Ludwig

Compelling Question	What does it mean to be perfect?
Common Core Standards	• CCSS.ELA-LITERACY.CCRA.R.2 • CCSS.ELA-LITERACY.CCRA.SL.1 • CCSS.ELA-LITERACY.CCRA.W.1 • NCSS—-4: Individual Development and Identity • NCSS Inquiry Arc—Dimension 4
Staging the Question	Read *The King and the Carpenters* by Farr and Tone

Supporting Question 1 (Before reading) What does it mean to be perfect?	Supporting Question 2 (During reading) What are the negative effects of trying to be perfect for Kayla in Too Perfect?	Supporting Question 3 (After reading) What are the differences between performance and mastery goals? Which type of goal do you think best defines your goals?
What does it mean to be perfect? How can one know when he or she is perfect? What does it mean to be perfect? Who sets the bar/expectation of what perfection is? Do you know someone who is perfect or close to perfect in school or athletics? What makes you say that? Are they perfect? Is being perfect a good goal to have? Why or why not? Can anyone ever be perfect?	How does Masie feel about Kayla at the beginning of the book? How does Kayla's success make Masie feel about herself? What negative impacts does Kayla's desire for perfection have on her life? Have you ever been affected by this desire for perfection? How does Masie's mother's try to make her feel about her performances? How does perfection relate to performance? How does perfection relate to mastery?	What are performance goals? What are mastery goals? Has your definition of perfection changed? How? What is more important: achieving performance goals or mastery goals? What is performance anxiety? Have you ever experienced it? How would you create descriptions on a SMART rubric to measure mastery or performance goal qualities?
Formative Performance Task	*Formative Performance Task*	*Formative Performance Task*
Define perfection Illustrate perfection Read the Introductory Internet Selection	Read the book: *Too Perfect* Complete graphic organizer listing performance goals and mastery goals found in the text	Create a rubric for mastery Compare and contrast your illustrations of perfection

Featured Sources	Featured Sources	Featured Sources
The King and the Carpenters (Farr and Tone, 1998).	*Too Perfect* by Trudy Ludwig	*The King and the Carpenters, Too Perfect,* and their parents' stories as resources to develop deep understanding about the results of mastery vs. performance goals.

Summative Performance Task	**Argument**	Think about Kayla. Was she performance oriented or mastery oriented?
	Extension	Identify an environment in which a person or organization emphasized performance rather than mastery for others. For example: The Little League Coach who only plays the "good" players in the championship game. Use your rubric to "inform the coach."
Taking Informed Action (Enrichment)		Have your parents tell you about a time when they felt they reached a level of perfection. Using your "rubric" score your parents' story. Explain to your parents the results of your interpretation of their perfection.

STAGING THE LESSON

When first reading the compelling question, the question seems simple enough. However, as one probes deeper into the understanding of what "perfection" really is, students should begin to realize that perfection means different things depending on context and audience and cannot be measured by a score. Teachers and parents should note that other texts might be used in the anticipatory set depending on the ability and comprehension level of the teacher and the geopolitical environment they teach in.

Each student will receive the compelling question and will brainstorm "how do you know when you are perfect?" and will illustrate what perfection looks like in the form of a picture. Groups of students will record their responses on chart paper and, once completed, perform a "gallery walk" to see other's responses and illustrations. When the students return to the whole class, learners will be probed to ascertain what information they gleaned from their walk.

Students will compare and contrast their findings with those of their classmates to internalize ideas that were consistent throughout the groups as well as those that were divergent. Ideally, throughout the students' discussion, commonalities will trigger realization of how society has shaped (and in some cases warped) our ideas about what perfection is, or should be. As the discussion moves on, students should begin to understand that perfection is unattainable.

Sophisticated students may mention that perfection is "setting a reasonable goal and reaching it. . . a picture of the sun setting when viewed at the beach." That in turn should bring up the concept of performance versus mastery. For groups that are less sophisticated or miss the bridge from a discussion of perfection to performance and mastery, they will perform a "sort" activity. Students performing the sort activity will be given a series of scenarios and will be asked to sort them into categories such as performance or mastery (see Table 6.2).

Students will then be introduced to *The King and the Carpenters* (Farr & Tone, 1998). Teachers have a variety of methods in their tool-boxes to read the story depending on the culture in their classroom. Some teachers may choose to have students read independently and silently, in partnerships, or small groups, or perhaps even modify the text and use it for reader's theater.

Once the story is read, teachers should *not* ask the students what the moral of the story is: "There is a big difference between naming hammers and pounding nails in a wall" (Farr, 1993). This is more to illustrate the differences between performance (naming hammers) and mastery (using hammers to create architecture that will stand the test of time).

Story summary: Once upon a time, there lived a king who had the best architecture in the land. His carpenters were *masters* at shaping wood and constructing buildings. The king decided to go to a "kings' conference" and share his wonderful kingdom.

The king finds that others kings do not believe him because he does not have proof (test scores of the carpenters). The king decides to validate what others believe and begins evaluating his carpenters via tests. The carpenters *perform* miserably, and the king focuses his efforts on getting better scores.

Scores begin to rise, as the emphasis in the kingdom becomes identifying correct test answers on tests rather than applying the tenets of proper building design and maintenance. Eventually, years later, he has the best scores in the land, but all too late finds his kingdom fallen into disrepair (after his balcony collapses under his weight and the weight of all the tests in his hands). At this point, students and teachers should chomp at the bit to begin the story.

THE READ-ALOUD: STORIES THAT STICK

The students are now ready to engage in the read-aloud exploring the story in whatever format that the teacher shares to read the story. Questions before, during, and after the reading are on the template and are provided merely as suggestions.

It is the belief of the authors that questions used to drive the reading are best created by the individual classroom teacher as part of the teachable moments that make read-aloud experiences come to life. More than likely, the suggestions will get you started and follow-up questions will arise in response to students' reactions.

SUMMATIVE PERFORMANCE TASKS

During this lesson, students will no doubt identify the differences between performance and mastery goals as well as the effects each can have on one's physical and mental state. The story should also help students develop a heightened awareness of groups and establishments within our society that places an emphasis on "performance perfection" rather than "mastery perfection." After the story, students might brainstorm ways in which to change the mindset of our schools, parents, and society.

While there are many ways to have students develop a deep understanding on the differences between performance and mastery goals, students may decide to reach out to a group or establishment that they feel perpetuates a "performance perfection" mindset. Perhaps students will write to a local children's sports organization that only plays its top athletes, rather than allowing all students time to play in the game.

Students might also decide to create a blog that highlights stories of "mastery perfection" and is shared with the school community. Modeling healthy, mastery goals will help create a shift within the culture of the school building and empower learners.

TAKING INFORMED ACTION

The mindset of education in today's world is markedly different from 30+ years ago. Student empowerment and setting reasonable goals are the wave of the future. Young learners are helping this wave become a reality, one fantastic example being youth like Adora Svitak. Ms. Svitak is a child prodigy who believes that kids should be kids. Not running around acting childish but being full of inspiring aspiration and hopeful thinking (Ted, 2010).

Svitak's ethos talks about children dreaming about perfection because "in order to make anything a reality you have to dream about it first" (Ted, 2010). Students should be encouraged to think of new ways to make the world a better place. The progression of this lesson allows students to make a difference in a world in which they understand.

Moving from their basic knowledge and dreams of what they believe "perfection" is to developing a more informed understanding of how it relates to the real world is key. Students can begin to fully understand this by bridging from *King and the Carpenters* through *Too Perfect* and developing a rubric and applying it to real-world examples.

After practice using their rubric, students are encouraged to extend this experience to the home by addressing the following prompt: *Have your parents tell you about a time when they felt they reached a level of perfection. Using your "rubric" score your parents' story. Explain to your parents the results of your interpretation of their perfection.*

The first two parts are simple enough: parents "tell a story" and students "evaluate the story." The third part can be problematic. Parents will want to hear the score, but may not be able to understand what the score truly means unless educated about the process of how the rubric was created.

Students should first introduce their experiences in answering the compelling question. What was discussed when identifying differences with perfection, performance, and mastery while completing the formative performance tasks? Learners are encouraged to discuss with parents their experiences in school.

Allowing parents to experience their child's development in understanding the differences and the importance of performance/perfection and mastery/perfection helps in understanding the child's rubric score for their experience. Students should ask their parents how they feel, not about the score but what the score represents through the use of the rubric. Students should also ask their parents if they would have chosen a different story now that they have not only seen the rubric but have also understood the process that creating the rubric entailed.

The compelling question that sparked this chapter has a vast number of possible answers. It is the experience that individuals take away from answering this question that is important. How can these experiences help make the world a better place?

Table 6.2. Scenario Sort

For a long time I ran an 8-minute mile. I recently decided I wanted to break it, so I set a goal for 7 minutes 55 seconds. Each day I followed a plan my coach had helped me create, running different distances and always pushing myself to work hard. Three weeks later, I did it!	For a long time I wanted to be fast because my friends are into running. Every time we race, I try to beat them. If I don't win, I run the next day for at least an hour. I get very nervous now before each race, but last week I finally came in first.
I have to study for my test tomorrow. I was told about the exam last week but I had softball practice and dance on Tuesday and Thursday. I am going to study for 3 hours tonight. I want to pass the test.	I found out that I have an exam next week. If I start to study every day for the exam starting today, I am sure that I will learn everything I need.
My coach said that I need to practice more for my lacrosse team if I want to get more playing time. I am going to invite my friends over for a game of catch today.	I spoke with my coach yesterday about getting more playing time. He said that I need to work on passing the ball. I am going to take my lacrosse stick and practice throwing and catching against the wall. I practiced for an hour today and will spend 30 minutes each day for the rest of the week. I will ask the coach to assess my progress and give me more suggestions next week.

Table 6.3. Examples from the Text: Performance versus Mastery Goals

Name: _____

Example of Performance Perfection	Example of Mastery Perfection	Describe the Impacts It Has on Characters	Page #

Table 6.4. Student-Created Mastery or Performance Goals Rubric

Descriptor	Very Much Like the Perfection Story	Like the Perfection Story but Not Totally	Only Slightly Like the Perfection Story	Not at All Like the Perfection Story
Students Create Description of a Goal That Embodies Performance Goal				
Students Create Description of a Goal That Embodies Performance Goal				
Students Create Description of a Goal That Embodies Mastery Goal				
Students Create Description of a Goal That Embodies Mastery Goal				
Level of Perfection Achieved— Attained or Unattainable				

Section II B: Building Hope: The Power of Hope to Create Your Best Future

Chapter 7

Hope Creators

The Power of Others

Rosie Revere, Engineer by Andrea Beaty and David Roberts

HOW THIS BOOK CONNECTS TO POSITIVE PSYCHOLOGY RESEARCH ON HOPE

This chapter lays the foundation for understanding the components that make up and maintain the psychological construct of *hope*. Rick Snyder of the University of Kansas pioneered hope research, and the standard bearer for that research most recently was Shane Lopez.

Sadly, Shane Lopez passed away shortly before the publication of this book, but the lessons that follow live on in Shane's memory. Shane asserted in numerous formats that man is the only animal that can imagine a future. Hope is the belief that individuals have control over the direction and quality of that future. Hope is not an inborn capacity but a way of thinking.

Most people think of hope as a synonym for wishful thinking. That colloquial hope is not the researched hope of positive psychology. C. R. Snyder, when investigating why people make excuses, found that some people do not make excuses but find their way around obstacles. Snyder defined the other side of excuses as *hope* and created instruments to measure the psychological construct hope.

These tests measured people's insight on the *ways* to circumnavigate obstacles and their *will* to go out that path that needs to be taken to get to that goal. Profound and extensive research efforts have linked higher hope with success in academics, athletics, traumatic injury, terminal illness, aging, and occupational success.

The two distinct parts that make up hope are formally referred to as *pathways* (the ways), in plain English what you have to do to shape a positive future (the way) and agency, the tenaciousness to carry out these pathways (the will). Of the two, research has revealed that agency, the will, is the most significant in predicting success.

Hope matters for students because the Gallop Poll reveals that hope is a better predictor of college completion than high school GPA, SAT, or ACT scores. The good news about hope is that it is a way of thinking and not an inborn character trait. If you can change your way of thinking, you can change your hope.

Hope is most dramatically affected by success and failure. Nothing builds hope like success, and nothing destroys hope quite as drastically as failure. When we meet Rosie, a gifted and passionate young inventor, we learn quickly how dramatically perceived failure can affect hope.

When Rosie's hat to keep the snakes off of one's head is laughed at by her beloved Uncle Fred, Rosie loses hope. Rosie temporarily keeps her dreams to herself and loses the will to invent, until meeting a great-great-aunt Rose. Aunt Rose inspires young Rosie to attempt to create a flying machine.

Although the dreamed-of flying machine crashes shortly to earth, Aunt Rose teaches young Rosie that failure is only the first step in success and needs to be viewed that way. What Rosie had thought of a "flop" becomes viewed as merely a first step on the way to success after coaching by Aunt Rose. This rediscovered and strengthened hope becomes a catalyst for change, and young Rosie goes on to inspire others and transform her class-room into a *hope factory*.

What is most intriguing about hope is the powerful role other people play in creating hope or crushing hope. Other people can help create hope or self-belief in us or, in other cases, can crush our self-belief. *Others* have the power to change the conversations in our heads, both positively and negatively.

It is important to use terminology to simplify the power of others and to provide a vocabulary for children to describe those roles. *Hope creator* is a great way to describe those people who build up our hope; hope creators are most needed when children are not successful and encouraging abilities and competency is in jeopardy. Research has documented the power of hope creators in the lives of successful people.

In this book, Aunt Rose appears when Rosie seems to have lost hope and convinces Rosie that past failures were really "raging successes." Aunt Rose is Rosie's *hope creator* when young Rosie most needs one. In a different direction, people can crush one's hope deliberately or unintentionally.

When Rosie's Uncle Fred laughs at Rosie's invention of a hat to keep snakes away, her uncle unknowingly acts a *hope crusher* and unintentionally crushes Rosie's hope and belief. Rosie's dream of being an inventor fades as her hope diminishes. This book is a perfect vehicle for teaching children about the role of others in the fragile, often changing nature of hope.

Important lessons are embedded in this simple story that has the power to teach children about the role of success or failure in creating hope. It shows the power of others to either maintain or crush hope in trying times. This lesson is significant for children, who must learn to recognize, seek out, and even become the hope creators in life.

It is equally important for children to recognize and mitigate the effects of those who crush hope in life. Research has revealed that struggling students often report that parents, intentionally or unintentionally, are the child's greatest hope crushers. That lesson is one that needs to be shared with parents as much as with children.

More detailed information on hope research is available for teachers and parents in the reference section in Chapter 20 of this book. These shared sources on hope include YouTube presentations, life-altering books applying the research to daily life, and a snapshot of the scholarly research from which the positive psychology supporting the chapter has been derived. Teachers are encouraged to dig deeper into developing a rich understanding of the research in order to strengthen the power and delivery of the lesson.

Lesson Design: *Rosie Revere, Engineer*
Jessica Ryan

Table 7.1.   The Power of Others: *Rosie Revere, Engineer* by Andrea Beaty and David Roberts

The Secret of Failing Well: *Rosie Revere, Engineer*		
Compelling Question	How do other people affect our hope?	
Common Core Standards	• CCSS.ELA-LITERACY.CCRA.R.2 • CCSS.ELA-LITERACY.CCRA.SL.1 • CCSS.ELA-LITERACY.CCRA.W.1 • NCSS—Theme 4: Individual Development and Identity • NCSS Inquiry Arc—Dimension 4	
Staging the Question	Play the video that features lyrics of Taylor Swift's "Shake It Off" and discuss how to react to other people's opinions.	
Supporting Question 1 *(Before reading)* What effects do the opinions of others have on you?	*Supporting Question 2* *(During reading)* What is a hope creator? What is a hope crusher?	*Supporting Question 3* *(After reading)* Who are the hope creators in your life?

Continued

Table 7.1. Continued

How do others impact how you feel? How do you react when other people have a negative response to your ideas? How do you react when people have a positive response to your ideas? What qualities does a role model have? Has someone in your life made you believe that you could do something that you thought you could not do? Has someone ever made you feel like you could not do something? What effect did this have on you?	Why do you think Rosie is trying to secretly create her inventions? How does Rosie feel when people laugh at her inventions? What evidence in the text led you to that conclusion? Why does Rosie care what other people think? Why did great-great-aunt Rose consider the cheese-copter crashing a "great flop"? How did great-great-aunt Rose change Rosie's thinking? What proof in the text supports your answer?	How would the story have changed if she really did "keep her dreams to herself"? How did great-great-aunt Rose support Rosie's dreams? Why did Rosie cheer on her classmates' failures? How has a role model inspired you? How can you motivate others?
Formative Performance Task	*Formative Performance Task*	*Formative Performance Task*
Students will actively listen to the lyrics of Taylor Swift's "Shake It Off" and discuss how to react to other people's negative opinions.	Throughout the book, students will "Turn and Talk" with a partner to discuss the answers to the supporting questions.	Students will write a personal narrative about a moment someone inspired them. During a follow-up lesson, students will then write about the same moment from the perspective of the hope creator.
Featured Sources	*Featured Sources*	*Featured Sources*
"Shake It Off" by Taylor Swift https://www.youtube.com/watch?v=nfWlot6h_JM	*Rosie Revere, Engineer* By Andrea Beaty and David Roberts	SMARTboard with audio

Summative Performance Task	**Argument**	Students will write a personal narrative from their perspective about a moment someone inspired them. Students will then write about the same event from the point of view of the person who inspired them.
	Extension	Upon reflecting on the historical note within *Rosie Revere, Engineer*, students will research another historical figure who inspired others besides Rosie the Riveter's "We can do it" attitude during World War II.
Taking Informed Action (Enrichment)		After sharing their personal narratives with their parents, students will brainstorm strategies to be hope creators. Students will create short video skits, where they can share these strategies.

STAGING THE LESSON

After listening to Taylor Swift's song "Shake It Off," students will discuss the message behind the song. Students will have the opportunity to conduct a close read of the lyrics to the song. During their close read, students will critically analyze and draw conclusions about the lyrics. Students will use the double-sided chart to record their conclusions and refer to their "thought prints" during the motivational discussion.

This song exemplifies the real challenge that both children and adults deal with. So often, students take to heart what other people say. When faced with a situation where thoughts and dreams are being tested, there are two choices that students have: either give credibility to others' opinions or "shake it off." This song naturally brings up discussion points on how to deal with negative comments from hope crushers.

Students can brainstorm strategies to successfully deal with negative comments. The power of hope can allow students to guide the inner conversation in their mind. By having a fixed mindset, the end result is already determined. On the other hand, hope stems from a growth mindset and the belief that anything can be changed with enough effort.

During the discussion of the song, the teacher should focus on how each student is unique and has different qualities. The lyrics in the song provide an opportunity for students to analyze the meaning behind them. Students can share how they can stand firm in individuality; they can support this with past examples of independence and confidence despite negativity and trying times.

It is vital for students to maintain a sense of self-belief even when doubted by *others*. The opinions of others should not thwart an individual's dreams. That's when the following questions arise: *How do you react when people have a negative response to an idea of yours? How do you react when people have a positive response to an idea of yours?* The crux of this discussion really has to do with how children perceive feedback from others and how this affects the conversations in their heads.

THE READ-ALOUD: STORIES THAT STICK

The students are now ready to engage in the read-aloud exploring the story in whatever format that the teacher chooses to share the story. Questions before, during, and after the reading are on the template and are provided merely as suggestions.

It is the belief of the authors that questions used to drive the reading are best created by the individual classroom teacher as part of the teachable moments that make read-aloud experiences come to life. More than likely, the suggestions will get you started and follow-up questions will arise in response to students' reactions.

SUMMATIVE PERFORMANCE TASKS

The assessment really seeks to have student understand and experience the core of our compelling question, *how do other people affect our hope?* This assessment allows students to reflect on a time when someone else has inspired them and positively changed their hope. By having a source of support, people are more likely to achieve dreams.

One person can tell students that they can conquer their fears, achieve the impossible, and get past those first few "great flops." Having just one person believe in a student will allow the student to believe in his or her own ability. Students are first going to write about that moment in a personal narrative. This will allow them to synthesize thoughts and emotions, and mirror the events within the book. Depending on the ability of the writer, students will include a strong lead, sensory details, "zoom in" on the main moment, dialogue, similes, metaphors, and a strong ending.

The next day, students will write about the same moment from the perspective of the hope creator. This will allow students to think of a situation from a different point of view. By thinking of the same situation from a different vantage point, the quality of empathy will be revealed in those who inspire others.

This writing gives teachers the opportunity to build in a lesson about character education. If students realize how and why others can build up hope and self-esteem rather than bring others down, perhaps they will learn to "stand and cheer" for others just as Rosie did. After students complete the writing assignment, they will reflect upon the differences between their two writing pieces.

The teacher should bring the discussion back to the essential question, *how do other people affect our hope?* From there, students should be further pushed to analyze how others can positively affect the conversation in one's heads.

Extension

Within *Rosie Revere, Engineer*, great-great-aunt Rose was based on Rosie the Riveter who encouraged women to join the workforce during World War II.

This is explained within the historical note. To extend the lesson within this book and bridge across the curriculum to social studies, students will research another historical figure who inspired others.

Students can use literature, informational texts, and the Internet to conduct research. After paraphrasing the information, they will create a "Museum of Motivators" bulletin board to share the insights gained. This can provide inspirational messages that others can benefit from long after the lesson's conclusion.

Argument

Students will create writing pieces that comply with the specific Common Core writing standards for their grade level. The ability to write a structured and detailed narrative is part of the Common Core Anchor Standards for all grade levels. Students are also writing from two different points of view, which makes the writing even more introspective.

TAKING INFORMED ACTION

A vital part of this lesson is not only what the students learn, but also how they can share the information with others. Students will share both versions of their personal narratives with their parents. This can give parents a time to reflect with their child on the importance of supporting dreams. Both the parents and students will brainstorm strategies and actors in the latter's lives that serve as hope creators.

This assignment will focus on the power of positively influencing the voices in other people's minds. Everyone has the power to inspire change in others for the better. Students will work with parents to create short video skits, where they can share these strategies. The videos can be accessed on the classroom website.

By creating QR codes, the links to the videos can be posted throughout the school. The QR codes can be accessed with a smartphone, a tablet, or a laptop that has a document camera. These easily accessible videos can serve as a reminder to other students to continue to be hope persuaders. This can serve as an appropriate teaching tool on the playground, in the hallway, in the classroom, or in the lunchroom.

The QR codes to the videos can also be easily distributed on flyers for other families to view and discuss. This will allow for students to act as informed citizens and make a difference by teaching others to be hope creators rather than hope crushers.

Figure 7.1. Video of Student Hope Homework

Chapter 8

Hope Crushers

Rediscovering Lost Hope

Emily's Art by Peter Catalanotto

HOW THIS BOOK CONNECTS TO POSITIVE PSYCHOLOGY RESEARCH ON HOPE

Emily's Art brings to life major understandings about hope that enable students to understand the effects of hope on emotion. For many in positive psychology, hope is often equated and sometimes considered interchangeable with self-efficacy. Although the distinctions are more aptly dealt with in the realm of positive psychology text than this venue, there is a vital distinction that students need to understand.

Hope levels, as pictured by C. R. Snyder, change continuously in a feedback loop that is dependent on the events that shape experience. Hope is a constantly changing perception and in this continually evolving and altered state based on experiences and *tied deeply into our emotions*. Students need to understand that feelings of happiness and self-worth may be tied into current levels of hope.

The best news about hope is that it is a way of thinking and not a character trait. Students need to know that at times they will feel extremely hopeful, competent, and satisfied. Failure or setbacks, unkind comments of others, may diminish hope, leaving a student feeling hopeless and depressed. Borrowing the name of a once-popular movie, the best way to describe hope is that *Hope Floats*. The most encouraging news that students need to absorb is that by merely changing their way of thinking lost hope can be rediscovered.

Experiences, both positive and negative, what others say, and even emotions can cause radical shifts in hope. In the story *Emily's Art*, an insensitive judge in an art contest is the source of the radical destruction of Emily's hope. Students need to learn how powerful words can be in building or destroying another's hope. The window on hope is the self-talk or the conversation in one's head that shares openly what one feels on an often-unconscious level.

C. R. Snyder saw this loop between hope and goals as a continuous one with some events sending positive feedback on goal pursuit, some sending negative messages, and others distracting from goal pursuit. *Emily's Art* provides an important teaching tool for students to understand that losses in hopes based on setbacks or unkind comments are normal and part of the nature of the feedback loop.

Kelly, Emily's friend, rekindles Emily's self-belief and students need to know that as easily as Emily's hope was lost, it can be reborn. Hope is most powerfully created by success, by key people who support us, and by a community that values our contributions. In the same way, hope can be lost through failure, by key people who do not encourage but disparage, and by a community that does not support individuals. This story can serve as the building block to creating school communities based on hope and making students ambassadors of hope.

This lesson builds on the previous lesson by revealing to students that hope is tied deeply into emotions. Hope is a source of not only the will to achieve a goal but also the happiness that makes attaining a goal fulfilling. This may be vital for students who are not meeting success and who are plagued by unhappiness and depression. Reinforcing the role that each individual can play in the hope of another is also a key understanding driving this lesson.

More detailed information on hope research is available for teachers and parents in the reference section in Chapter 20 of this book. These shared sources on hope include YouTube presentations, life-altering books applying the research to daily life, and a snapshot of the scholarly research from which the positive psychology supporting the chapter has been derived. Teachers are encouraged to dig deeper into developing a rich understanding of the research in order to strengthen the power and delivery of the lesson.

Lesson Design: *Emily's Art*
Danielle Rosenberg

Table 8.1. Hope Crushers: Rediscovering Lost Hope: *Emily's Art* by Peter Catalanotto

Compelling Question	How does hope affect our emotions?
Common Core Standards	• CCSS.ELA-LITERACY.CCRA.R.2 • CCSS.ELA-LITERACY.CCRA.SL.1 • CCSS.ELA-LITERACY.CCRA.W.1 • NCSS—Theme 4: Individual Development and Identity • NCSS Inquiry Arc—Dimension 4
Staging the Question	Tell a story of hope being crushed, and the students will identify the hope creator and hope crusher from the story.

Supporting Question 1 (Before reading) What effect can a hope crusher have on your emotions?	Supporting Question 2 (During reading) What effect did the hope crusher have on Emily in Emily's Art?	Supporting Question 3 (After reading) What can you do if your hope is crushed, and what strategies do you have to keep hope alive?
What is a hope crusher? What event or person crushed my personal hope in the story I just shared with you? Why was my hope crushed? What evidence supports your determination that my hope was crushed? Was hope restored? How? Or What event or person crushed hope in the story we just viewed on YouTube? Why was hope crushed? What evidence supports your determination that hope was crushed? Was hope restored? How?	How can you describe Emily in the beginning of the story? What evidence do you have that Emily liked painting? How do you know? Who was Emily's hope crusher? How do you know her hope was crushed? How did Emily feel after losing the art contest and having her hope crushed? How was Emily's hope created again? Have you ever had an experience in which your hope was lost? Was it restored? How?	What did Emily realize at the end of the story? Did the conversation in Emily's head change after her hope was crushed? If so, how? Was Emily happier in the beginning of the story or at the end? How do you know? Did you ever feel like Emily in any way? Do you know anyone like Emily? How can we be hope creators and not hope crushers in the lives of others?
Formative Performance Task	Formative Performance Task	Formative Performance Task
The teacher presents a personal story about having hope crushed or a YouTube example. The teacher asks questions to get the students thinking about the characteristics of a hope crusher/creator. Students will participate in a collaborative discussion.	Students will respond to the supporting questions at key points during the text.	Students will interview a partner about a time their hope was crushed. They will identify the change in the conversation in their head based on the experience.

Continued

Table 8.1.   Continued

Featured Sources	Featured Sources	Featured Sources
Open Ended-Teacher Choice	*Emily's Art* by Peter Catalanotto	Interview worksheet https://www.powtoon.com/home/

Summative Performance Task	**Argument**	Students will interview classmates about hope creators and crushers in their own lives. They will report findings as a class and write a passage in their notebooks answering the compelling question based on their interviews.
	Extension	Students will interview their parents about a time their hope was crushed and create a PowToon presentation to share this with the class.
Taking Informed Action (Enrichment)	Students will write a class book, *Rediscovering Lost Hope*, and share it with other classes in the school and the world.	

STAGING THE LESSON

This lesson begins by simply posing the questions, "What is hope? Does hope float? Can we rediscover our hope if we lose it? What effect do hope gains or losses have on our happiness? Although these questions might be a review, if the previous lesson has been completed, it is an ideal way to check student understanding. There may be a large variety of answers, stories, and examples given by students.

Hope can mean many things to many different people, but this lesson deals with the question of lost hope and hope found again. The compelling question not only involves how it affects our emotions and sense of well-being. Students need to gain the understanding of how hope can be restored when an individual loses hope. Hope can be crushed in many ways, but no matter which way, the damage is always devastating and discouraging for children.

By asking or reviewing with students what or who creates and crushes hope in their life, the teacher can reinforce the big idea that hope goes up and down in students' lives. The complexity of staging this lesson enters when you ask students to relate personal experiences of lost hope that negatively changed their self-talk. Self-talk is best referred to as the *conversation in their heads.*

Many students will first begin to understand the nature of self-talk from the staging. Conversations in our head vary, but making students aware of the powerful effect of self-talk on behavior and *emotion.* Hopeful conversations in their head might make students believe anything is possible. These conversations arise from success and encouragement.

When failure or others crush belief about an individual's own ability and competence, the conversation in his or her head changes. Students often begin to internalize and believe what others say. Instead of recognizing talents and areas in which one might excel, students begin to lose hope and belief. Students can lose *hope*, and thus their ability to shape their own future.

When teachers share stories or use examples from personal life, it allows students to see teachers in a different light. Suddenly, teachers become real people and not just adults in front of the room each day. The personal story of the teacher or a selected YouTube video also allows for students to create deeper meanings and connections because students begin to make connections between their emotions and hope.

For this lesson, the teacher's story should describe a time in life when hope was crushed. The story should have a problem and solution. There should be a noticeable difference from the beginning of the story when hope was crushed, and the modeled story should provide a resolution when their hope was reestablished. This story allows for students to process and sequence what occurs in the read-aloud and how it relates to Emily's self-talk.

If the teacher is not comfortable in sharing a personal story, there are numerous clips on YouTube that highlight the depths of despair that an individual encountered before ultimate triumph. These clips are another way to stage the lesson by laying a groundwork that enables students to connect the story they will read to an existing pathway and ultimately to their own lives.

With older children, this is an ideal time to ask students to begin to reflect on times when their hope was crushed and then restored. This depends on the age and maturity of the class and may result in deeply personal stories emerging. Teachers need to use judgment on this application with a deep knowledge of the maturity and trust in the room. However, if and when students share their stories of lost hope, it truly cements neurological connections that make the learning permanent.

By asking students to recall details from the story to answer questions, you are enabling them to make connections and develop a deeper understanding for themselves about what it means to have the conversations in their heads changed (self-talk). These discussions also create a collaborative community among students, which can also bring light to clearer understanding of the fragile nature of hope. *Hope floats.*

THE READ-ALOUD: STORIES THAT STICK

The students are now ready to engage in the read-aloud exploring the story in whatever format that the teacher shares to read the story. Questions before, during, and after the reading are on the template and are provided merely as suggestions.

It is the belief of the authors that questions used to drive the reading are best created by the individual classroom teacher as part of the teachable moments that make read-aloud experiences come to life. More than likely, the suggestions will get you started and follow-up questions will arise in response to students' reactions.

SUMMATIVE PERFORMANCE TASK

When students are given the opportunity to talk with one another without a teacher listening to their conversation, ideas begin to flourish. For the summative performance task, students will interview one another about hope crushers and creators in their lives and moments of change based on pervious experiences.

Students will ask one another about a time when hope may have been crushed, how it made them feel, feelings before hope was crushed, and how thinking and self-talk changed during this time. Students will follow this line of questioning seeking the ways in which hope was rediscovered.

This activity requires students to reflect on past scenarios and look at them in a new way. Students also have the chance to understand and speak with peers in a different manner as well, a more personal one. As students open up to one another about these moments in their lives, they begin connecting on many levels: with the lesson, with each other, and with Emily from the story. These are connections that will come to light as students dive into discussion.

It is important for students to work with one another collaboratively. The idea of an interview is also important because it allows students to take the main focus off their personal experience and focus on someone else's feelings. Using these interviews as evidence, students will answer the compelling question.

Extension

Application of classroom lessons to the outside world is incredibly crucial. The connections made from lessons to a student's home life truly bridge the gap between home and school and allow the lesson to come full circle. When students can discuss learning in the school day with someone at home, they are not only reinforcing what is learned but are also making newer and deeper connections to the lesson.

This lesson's extension is similar to the summative performance task. Students are asked to interview their families about hope, hope crushers, hope creators, and the conversations in their head. Families may have different points of views about such topics, which only broaden a student's knowledge. Students are also asked to find out the hope crushers and creators in their lives. This can also broaden their understanding and help them identify the fragile nature of hope.

Students will use the website *PowToon* as a fun way to share their stories and create a deeper understanding of the idea that hope is changeable and fragile. Connecting their experiences and feelings to their parents' experiences is a powerful way to connect this concept to their lives beyond the lesson through technology.

TAKING INFORMED ACTION

It is not satisfactory to teach a lesson and let the learning end there. Teachers must provide an outlet for students to apply what they have learned from the lesson and share it with the world. As students apply their knowledge to authentic audiences, they create deeper connections. This lesson culminates by providing students the opportunity to create a book entitled *Rediscovering Lost Hope*. There are no guidelines for this book and what is to be included or not included. In essence, students are given full creative reign in whatever format to share their personal stories and understandings about rediscovered hope.

This story sharing is a vehicle through which students can shine and truly use and expand their knowledge of the lesson. This is also an engaging manner for students to share their learning with others. After students create their book, they will share their book with other classes in the school; thus they will be becoming hope creators in a civic manner that brings the National Council for Social Studies Standards to life.

Chapter 9

Maintaining Hope

Finding Your Best Self

Stand Tall, Molly Lou Melon by Patty Lovell and David Catrow

HOW THIS BOOK CONNECTS TO POSITIVE PSYCHOLOGY
RESEARCH ON HOPE

The book *Stand Tall, Molly Lou Melon* reveals to young readers the continuing challenge that maintaining hope can pose in the face of what C. R. Snyder and other hope researchers have referred to as *stressors*. Stressors are any obstacles that come between an individual and his or her goal. In the previous books, there were obstacles in obtaining the goal, but they were singular in nature. This story will segue naturally and logically into the next section on *grit*, which will lead into perseverance, which arises from passion for a goal that enables one to overcome overwhelming *stressors*.

In *Stand Tall, Molly Lou Melon*, the stressors that Molly Lou faces are constant and continuing. There is not a single obstacle but a continuing series of challenges, and Molly Lou must obtain self-belief in the face of stressors that each has the power to destroy will. Molly Lou is never deterred by the threats to her self-belief and hope. Molly Lou's story provides a powerful example on how self-belief can be held to even in the face of continuing stressors.

What enables Molly Lou to maintain hope is her strong foundation of self-belief, never being deterred from her belief, even in the face of bullying. The lessons in this book are ideal for discussing the need for maintaining hope even in adverse situations and situations in which an individual is bullied.

What is shared with students is the follow-up activity in which students as a class can create a PATH (Planning Alternative Tomorrows with Hope) plan for addressing a goal. For students not as strong as Molly Lou, this plan can be helpful in anticipating stressors and enrolling those people and resources to overcome obstacles.

PATH plans and enables a group or class to chart actions that view progress and share a vision that views hope as a way to create brighter tomorrows. This template map process is recommended in the teacher resources section in Chapter 20. Ideas connecting the research driving this chapter are derived from this program.

The PATH plans will enable students to make hope-based plans for class projects that enable students to employ all of their understanding about hope, stressors, and goals to accomplish a goal. Students begin to understand that hope must be maintained over time if they are to live out their dreams for tomorrow. The template at the conclusion of this actually lays the groundwork for grit.

More detailed information on hope research is available for teachers and parents in the reference section in Chapter 20 of this book. These shared sources on hope include YouTube presentations, life-altering books applying the research to daily life, and a snapshot of the scholarly research from which the positive psychology supporting the chapter has been derived. Teachers are encouraged to dig deeper into developing a rich understanding of the research in order to strengthen the power and delivery of the lesson.

Lesson Design: *Stand Tall, Molly Lou Melon*
Elisabetta Bavaro

Table 9.1.   Finding Your Best Self: *Stand Tall, Molly Lou Melon* by Patty Lovell and David Catrow

Compelling Question	How can we maintain hope in the face of *stressors?*
Common Core Standards	• CCSS.ELA-LITERACY.CCRA.R.2 • CCSS.ELA-LITERACY.CCRA.SL.1 • CCSS.ELA-LITERACY.CCRA.W.1 • NCSS—Theme 4: Individual Development and Identity • NCSS Inquiry Arc—Dimension 4
Staging the Question	• Think of a time when you were your best self, your true self. Think of a time when you were stressed. • Think, pair, and share these moments with a classmate. Use your five senses to describe this moment in as much detail as possible • Students will complete templates *You're Stressing Me Out* and *The Best Me for All to See.*

Supporting Question 1 (Before reading) What are the stressors in your life?	Supporting Question 2 (During reading) How does Molly Lou combat stressors in Stand Tall, Molly Lou Melon?	Supporting Question 3 (After reading) How can you create a shield of resilience to combat stressors in your life?

Who was there with you?
Where were you?
What specifically were you doing?
How did it feel to believe in yourself?
Why do you consider this moment the best example of your true self/best self?
What does the word stress mean to you?
Who and what are some examples of "stressors" in your life?
Why do you consider these stressors?

If Molly Lou Melon were to create her own *The Best Me for All to See* photo frame, what attributes would she include?
Can you see yourself as the main character of this book at this point in the story?
How do you think Molly Lou will react to the "stressors" she will encounter in her "new life?"
Are these reactions similar to what you encountered when confronted by the "stressors" indicated on your *You're Stressing Me Out* photo frame?
Can Molly Lou maintain her self-belief in the face of stressors?

How does seeing your best self help you in the face of stressors?
What were the key components Molly Lou possessed that helped her defy the doubt and believe in herself?
What helped her break through the "stressors" she faced?

How did it feel to be stressed?
How have you reacted to the "stressors" in your life?
What effect did they have on your self-belief?
At any time were you able to overcome these stressors, and if so, how? What steps did you take?
Why do you consider this moment the best example of your stressed self?
Are these words a collage representing a life that is one of successes (best self) or failures (stressed self)?

Why doesn't Molly Lou tell someone about what Ronald is doing to her so that the "stressors" stop?
How does Molly Lou know to believe in herself and not turn way in "defeat"?
Why didn't Molly Lou change herself to "fit in" with her new classmates and her new school?
What does Ronald hope for with each encounter with Molly Lou?
What do you notice about the outcomes for each event?
Is Ronald the character that they can identify with most in the story?
Is there anyone in your life that you would write a thank-you letter to just like Molly Lou Melon did at the end of the book?

What helps you break through the "stressors" you face/encounter?

Continued

Table 9.1.   Continued

Formative Performance Task	Formative Performance Task	Formative Performance Task
Teacher poses questions encouraging students to share their Best Self and Stressed Self experiences. Think, pair, and share. Students create *The Best Me for All to See* and *You're Stressing Me Out* photo frames.	Students respond to the above questions at key points in the story.	Create: My Shield of Resilience Listen to: "Fight Song" by Rachel Platten "Roar" by Katy Perry "Firework" by Katy Perry "I Lived" by One Republic

Featured Sources	Featured Sources	Featured Sources
Photo frames: *The Best Me for All to See!* *You're Stressing Me Out!*	*Stand Tall, Molly Lou Melon* Written by Patty Lovell and illustrated by David Catrow	10 Strategies for "The New Resilient You!" My Shield of Resilience Lyrics to songs: "Fight Song" by Rachel Platten "Roar" by Katy Perry "Firework" by Katy Perry

Summative Performance Task	**Argument**	Write a first-person narrative that depicts an example of a time in which students maintained (or did not maintain) their self-belief in the face of stressors. OR Students will answer the compelling question in a Common Core opinion essay.
	Extension	Students will share with their parents their shield and have their parents create a similar shield.
Taking Informed Action (Enrichment)	*Understand*: A person's character takes shape throughout his or her life regardless of age or gender. The successes and/or failures in life can be viewed like the people in our lives. While some encourage us, others are the stressors that crush our hope and belief that we can achieve our goals. Nevertheless, if we change the voice in our head and have a growth mindset, then we see a world of possibilities and a network of resources. We can view supporters like an embrace, surrounding us with hope and empowering us to be resilient and confident and internalize that when we are our best self, we are indeed our true self, which will ultimately be inspiring to others. *Assess*: Determine how common individuals can take proactive and collaborative approaches in the real world toward maintaining their self-belief in the face of stressors as they achieve a goal. *Act*: Students will create a Defy the Doubt PATH and an awareness campaign to encourage others in and outside of their community to proactively maintain self-belief in the face of stressors.	

STAGING THE LESSON

The inquiry lesson begins with the students internalizing the compelling question, *can we maintain our self-belief in the face of stressors?* Through the inquiry process, students will have an opportunity to build upon their initial answers to this question as they dive deeper with scaffolded questions. It is important for students to have a clear foundation of the hope cycle being presented and an understanding of an array of possible outcomes and perspectives that can come to fruition as a result of this inquiry lesson.

Students' initial response to the compelling question regardless of age, background, gender, and ability will prove to be simple yet intriguing. A widely viewed reply to the compelling question can be one of optimism: "yes, you can maintain your self-belief in the face of stressors." Yet, students may also answer the compelling question by possibly taking on the point of view that "yes, we can maintain our self-belief in the face of stressors, but it would probably be hard for someone to do without some type of support system."

Alternatively, other students may respond with a pessimistic viewpoint simply because the key vocabulary of self-belief and stressors echo in their ears resulting in a quick premise that even though there is a will and a possible way, it would be a waste of time and any attempts would be futile. Either way, these initial answers allow the teacher to take a sneak peek and gauge the emotional temperature of the class. This discussion should help the teacher see those who view themselves successful and those who perceive themselves as failures in the face of challenges.

There are a variety of avenues to explore once students take a beginning stance on the compelling question. Students will undoubtedly want to discuss and express personal experiences of successes and failures and possibly learn that a failure in their eyes is an asset or a success to another. This type of discussion will naturally take place and possibly begin a healthy exchange among students.

This initial engagement activity provides students with the essence of the book by simply asking them to recall and reflect on experiences growing up. These experiences can be early memories from childhood or events and encounters that have happened recently and are expressed as representations of their best self and of their stressed self. The hands-on approach of drawing on prior knowledge allows students to take ownership in and of the inquiry lesson.

Suggesting that students visualize themselves in these vivid life scenes by using their five senses helps them validate this successful time because they were demonstrating their best self and realize what, on the surface, caused them to be unsuccessful or fail because they were exhibiting a stressed self. Appropriately posing probing questions within the activity can help crystalize past positive experiences. (Where were you? Who was there with you? What specifically were you doing? How did it feel to believe in yourself? Why do you consider this moment the best example of your true self/best self?)

On the other side of the equation, questions can also probe the darker side of their efforts? (What does the word *stress* mean to you? Who and what are some examples of "stressors" in your life? Why do you consider these stressors? How did it feel to be stressed? How have you reacted to the "stressors" in your life? What effect did they have on your self-belief? At any time were you able to overcome these stressors? If so, how? What steps did you take? Why do you consider this moment the best example of your stressed self?)

This activity allows descriptive details to emerge once again showing how this inquiry lesson directly connects to them and impacts the academic, social, and emotion sectors of their life. However, verbalizing these experiences is only the preliminary part of this portion of the staging of the lesson, where students merely scratch the surface of the essence of the book and its central message.

Therefore, opting to seeing what makes us our best selves and stressed selves as well as internalizing and coming to terms those experiences/conflicts is the challenging high dive or jump that few are willing to take and that is why having students partake in the creation of *The Best Me for All to See* and *You're Stressing Me Out* photo frames is a necessary step. It is a concrete indicator of their self-reflection and self-expression.

At this point, students can create a template that seeks to analyze the factors in their life that are actually stressing them out. In order to help students, it might be best to first create a template of stressors (Figure 9.1) in their lives that were first identified by the students in the initial discussions.

Students can then integrate their own feelings on chart (Figure 9.2) similar to this one. This chart pictorially represents for students the events in their lives that provide stress for them personally. This truly enables them to understand stressors in the best spirit of C. R. Snyder and Shane Lopez.

Students will now be provided with a list of attributes list (Figure 9.3) that arose from the initial brainstorming of the class. Feel free to borrow this list or create your own.

Using this chart, students will place the concepts that best define their beliefs about their individual attributes to be employed in combatting stressors. Students will begin to understand that to overcome the stressors in their lives, they will need to employ character strengths.

Students will create collages of the "Best Me for All to See" (Figure 9.4). These collages enable students to take a step back and ask a closing thought-provoking question: Are these words a collage representing a life that is one of successes (best self) or failures (stressed self)? As a result of this query, students can continue moving toward developing their comprehensive response to the compelling question.

The staging of the lesson portion of the inquiry seamlessly flows into the introduction and reading of the book simply because it is about a girl who believes in herself and exclaims to the world in each challenge she faces that because she is true to herself, here is *The Best Me for All to See*.

STRESSORS

Family: For example, siblings, friends
Classmates
Mother Nature
Change in surroundings or environment
Change in routine/schedule
Health
Time
Performance tasks:
School
Classmates
Reading
Writing
Math
Speaking
Homework
Schoolwork-projects
Concerts
Sports
Fear of failure
Pressure

The Unknown

Bavaro ©

Figure 9.1.   Stressors

Figure 9.2.   You're Stressing Me Out

The Best Me for All to See
Attributes List

Accepting	Eager	Peaceful
Adaptive	Easy-going	Persevere
Affectionate	Enthusiastic	Polite
Altruistic	Fair	Prepared
Ambitious	Faithful	Productive
Articulate	Flexible	Resilient
Assertive	Friendly	Respectful
Capable	Funny	Responsible
Caring	Generous	Sincere
Charismatic	Gentle	Self-Sacrificing
Charming	Honest	Thoughtful
Cheerful	Hopeful	Trustworthy
Clever	Hard Working	Understanding
Committed	Humorous	Visionary
Compassionate	Imaginative	Wise
Conscientious	Independent	
Considerate	Intelligent	
Cooperative	Kind	
Courageous	Logical	
Creative	Loveable	
Curious	Loyal	
Daring	Mature	
Decisive	Observant	
Determined	Optimistic	
Dependable	Organized	
Diligent	Patient	

Bavaro ©

Figure 9.3. Attributes List

Figure 9.4. The Best Me for All to See

THE READ-ALOUD: STORIES THAT STICK

The students are now ready to engage in the read-aloud exploring the story in whatever format that the teacher chooses to share the story. Questions before, during, and after the reading are on the template and are provided merely as suggestions.

It is the belief of the authors that questions used to drive the reading are best created by the individual classroom teacher as part of the teachable moments that make read-aloud experiences come to life. More than likely, the suggestions provided can get you started and follow-up questions will arise in response to students' reactions.

SUMMATIVE PERFORMANCE TASKS

As we all know, students' learning styles vary and many students may view creating a summative performance as a possible "stressor." Yet, we must think of the Molly Lou Melon inside all of us and not turn away from this opportunity in disguise but rather embrace it simply, because it will make the inquiry and life lessons taught richer and make them much more purposeful as well as meaningful.

Using the following template (Figure 9.5) or one of your own, students can fill out a shield of resilience entitled "The New Resilient You!" This shield will define their resilience in the center of the shield and their character strengths on the outside of the shield. This action clearly links the children with Molly Lou and arms the children with the needed resilience to confront obstacles that make up their personal stressors.

Students will read the *Time* magazine (June 1, 2015) article on resilience, "The New More Resilient You." Using the ten strategies adapted directly from the article, students will draw or write in three of the resilience strategies in the center of the shield.

1. Develop a core set of beliefs that nothing can shake.
2. Try hard to find meaning in whatever stressful thing has happened.
3. Try to maintain a positive outlook.
4. Take cues from someone who is especially resilient.
5. Don't run from things that care me: face them.
6. Be quick to reach out for support when things go haywire.
7. Learn new things as often as I can.
8. Find and exercise routine that I'll stick to.
9. Don't beat myself up or dwell on the past.
10. Recognize what makes me uniquely strong and own it.

THE NEW RESILIENT YOU

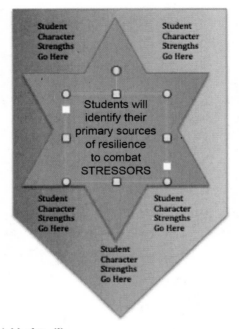

Figure 9.5. My Shield of Resilience

Based on their previous work on the *Best of Me for All to See* sheet, students then will write their character strengths on the outside of the shield. This completed shield can serve as a prewriting strategy arming students with relevant and thoughtful evidence to support final writing assessments.

To increase motivation and connections, students can fill out the sheet while listening to empowering and uplifting songs that could include "Fight Song" by Rachel Platten, "Roar" by Katy Perry, "Firework" also by Katy Perry, or "I Lived" by One Republic. The shield of resilience that students create is the key to harnessing strengths and self-belief to combat the stressors that they have identified to begin the lesson.

Argument/Extension

In order to extend the lesson into the home, students will share their shield of resilience with their parents. After teaching about stressors and character strengths, parents will create their own personal shield, which they will share with their children. Students will present their parents' shields to the class and create a bulletin board of parent and child shields.

At this state in the lesson segment, students have more than enough concrete evidence to support a sophisticated and informed response to the compelling question, *can we maintain our self-belief in the face of stressors?* Fusing all the knowledge students possess, information generated while they traveled (through various emotions, processes, realizations about themselves) and insights into how vital a role these elements play in their own lives, students can address the compelling question using specific claims and relevant evidence from the inquiry lesson all the while acknowledging competing views.

It should be encouraged that students craft a narrative or an essay to answer the compelling question. This approach or forum allows students to form a thesis and support it with a treasure chest full of evidence. This assignment fulfills the argument requirement but if we want the lesson to resonate in the real world another assignment might also culminate the lessons.

TAKING INFORMED ACTION

Transfer, shift application, relevance, purpose, meaning, whatever words a teacher might choose to use is the ultimate assessment of whether or not the inquiry life lesson was internalized. Bringing what was learned in the classroom out into the real world is a contagious type of learning that teachers all hope for.

Sparking the idea and igniting the flame of a concept learned about in school merely scratches the surface and only begins to show the true power the domino effect can have. The various factors in life—successes and failures as well as people we encounter, the stressors, the persuaders, the hope crushers, and vicarious others—all make up a culture that we live in daily. So it should come as no surprise that we see the youth, students, as ambassadors of hope and resilience to the world.

Although students may not all have the courage to empower themselves, they often encourage and remind us educators to be hopeful, resilient, and our best selves. That is why students are the best couriers of this important message and pathway of life. With each performance task in this inquiry, students have gathered information and have created a mindset map as to how to maintain self-belief and defy doubt.

That is why involving and immersing students in an infectious taking informed action with the world is crucial. Devising an effective and collaborative plan of action with their family, school, and/or community makes this practice of mindset permanent.

PATH is a planning and problem-solving process created by Jack Pearpoint, John O'Brien, and Marsha Forest to help students visualize and achieve a goal that brings to life a dream. More direction and information is available in the life-changing book *PATH: Planning Alternative Tomorrows with Hope* by Jack Pearpoint, John O'Brien, and Marsha Forest in the resources for students at the end of the book in Chapter 20.

The planning template (Figure 9.6) is an interactive navigation device that allows all that are involved to be explorers and discoverers of a desirable future or goal all the while learning and realizing that when working together, we are ultimately better. However, should a teacher choose to engage in this process, obtaining the book is a must.

With the students armed with an individual strategy to overcome stressors, PATH becomes the ideal process for the class to identify a goal and engage in a PATH group process to chart and achieve that group goal. Students can begin by creating a personally designed representation of the template in Figure 9.6 as a class. Similar to a way a class charter or mission statement begins, students should identify a goal and envision a desired future, filling in the chart with defined timelines.

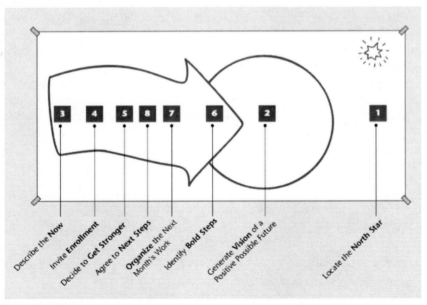

Figure 9.6. PATH Planning Template

With the goal established, students can use the template to strategically plan explicit steps to achieving that goal or vision. The process anticipates stressors and deals with them collaboratively as a group. As the process unfolds, the class may present a visual schematic of this on a bulletin board outside of their classrooms to share their learning with the entire school community.

Another avenue to explore that bridges the home and school connection is a parent workshop. The concept here is to invite parents into the class and have the students along with their parents to craft a family plan to achieve a goal using a PATH template in the positive psychology introduction. Since this template lays out a strategy for overcoming stressors in pursuing a goal, this is an excellent way to integrate the learning into the home.

Allowing the students to be at the forefront of their learning experience is vital. Being involved and transferring that information is enlightening for the student (now the teacher) and the other learners involved. Through this informed action transition, students can realize that all the components discovered in the inquiry lesson can be applied in the real world, where there can be moments of setbacks, fast-forwards, standstills, and quicks, but there is always progress toward the goal.

Sections II C: Cultivating Grit: Passion and Perseverance for Long-Term Goals

Chapter 10

The Roots of Grit

Deliberate Practice over Natural Ability

Salt in His Shoes by Deloris Jordan and Roslyn M. Jordan

HOW THIS BOOK CONNECTS TO POSITIVE PSYCHOLOGY RESEARCH ON GRIT

The book *Salt in His Shoes* provides the perfect introduction into the researched construct of grit. This story, sharing the early challenges of renowned Michael Jordan, has the power to dramatically challenge student perceptions of talent and success. The greatness of Michael Jordan is well known to all students, but the fact that he struggled to attain that greatness and had doubts about his ability may not be known.

Michael Jordan initially believes talent is inborn and can best be measured by height and natural talent, but a young Jordan soon learns that hard work and passion for the game is the source of greatness. This is the perfect introduction to grit, because it builds on growth mindset, hope, and provides a powerful lesson on the power of effort over inborn capacity.

At the start of the story, Michael fully believes that success in basketball originates from size. This belief comes from the fact that he is bullied and belittled for being too small. Only after the wisdom imparted by his father suggests that basketball talent may arise more from the hard work than size does Michael come to the realization that his hard work is the key to success and not his size.

Angela Duckworth is the pioneering researcher behind the grit concept, and this research is arguably the most popular research in positive psychology research today. Duckworth's groundbreaking effort began with creating

85

a measure that identified two elements that define grit: passion for a goal and perseverance needed to attain that goal.

The acclaim for the concept, named for the movie *True Grit*, arose when Duckworth's measure best predicted who would survive at West Point, in National Spelling Bees and in general measures of success in life. Based on her research, captivating TED talks, and now a *New York Times* best seller, *Grit: Passion and Perseverance for the Goal*, grit has captured the imagination of the education world and America. Grit has become the most talked about and debated positive psychology construct in America today.

The book *Salt in His Shoes* is a great introduction to grit; the story presents the idea that what makes us great is not an inborn capacity but effort for a long-term goal that we are passionate about. After the reading, the elements of passion for a goal and persevering over time to achieve that goal can be made clear by the example of Michael Jordan's life. The picture books that follow will deal with both passion and perseverance with greater specificity on the elements of grit.

In studying greatness, Duckworth proposes that deliberate practice, working at your craft in a very specific and directed manner, is what separates those who will go on to the greatest success. Deliberate practice involves working hard at what you need to improve on, seeking feedback, and responding to feedback, and has been described by Duckworth as not always fun. This focused and directed practice is not a process that many will endure.

What makes students endure directed practice is the passion they possess for the goal that they seek. Michael Jordan has an undeniable passion for basketball that was on display for the world for decades. This passion made possible the deliberate practice that gave rise to his renown. *Salt in His Shoes* opens the discussion on what makes us great in a simple manner and has the power to have students recognize that perseverance is a result of how badly an individual wants a goal.

More detailed information on grit research is available for teachers and parents in the reference section in Chapter 20 of this book. These shared sources on grit include YouTube presentations, life-altering books applying the research to daily life, and a snapshot of the scholarly research from which the positive psychology supporting the chapter has been derived. Teachers are encouraged to dig deeper into developing a rich understanding of the research in order to strengthen the power and delivery of the lesson.

Lesson Design: *Salt in His Shoes*
AnnMarie Pagano and Breanna Podmore

Table 10.1. Deliberate Practice over Natural Ability: *Salt in His Shoes* by Deloris Jordan and Roslyn M. Jordan

Compelling Question Standards	What makes someone great? • CCSS.ELA-LITERACY.CCRA.R.2 • CCSS.ELA-LITERACY.CCRA.SL.1 • CCSS.ELA-LITERACY.CCRA.W.1 • NCSS—Theme 4: Individual Development and Identity • NCSS Inquiry Arc—Dimension 4
Staging the Question	Brainstorm traits of people considered to be great. Examine a case study to discover parallels with the story to be read and with the researched roots of grit.

Supporting Question 1 (Before reading) What makes someone great?	*Supporting Question 2 (During reading)* What does Michael Jordan discover about greatness in* Salt in His Shoes?	*Supporting Question 3 (After reading)* What was the source of Michael's greatness and what will be the source of greatness in your life?
What makes someone great? Is it a natural ability that we are born with? Or a result of hard work and dedication?	What does Michael think that will make him better at basketball? Does height make a basketball player great? Do you think his mom's advice will work? What does Michael's dad say that changes his mind about giving up?	Did Michael have natural ability? Did that alone enable him to be great? What did Michael Jordan do to become so great? What was the turning point?
Formative Performance Task	*Formative Performance Task*	*Formative Performance Task*
Teacher presents students with questions about what makes a person great to elicit student views on hard work and effort. Students are then presented with a case study about a student who has natural ability that has not been fostered, which results in the student being cut from his school soccer team. Students are asked to complete a series of questions about the case study.	Students engage in collaborative discussion while the teacher reads them a book and asks questions based on the book.	Students watch a YouTube Video about Michael Jordan's devastation about being cut from his high school basketball team and his response.
Featured Sources	*Featured Sources*	*Featured Sources*
Case Study: Carlos Rodriguez	*Salt in His Shoes* by Deloris Jordan and Roslyn M. Jordan	YouTube Video: https://www.youtube.com/watch?v=1k2uD-P3Z3Y

Continued

Table 10.1.   Continued

Summative Performance Task	**Assignment**	Students will retell the story of Michael Jordan to their parent(s). Students will ask their parents about which athlete he or she holds to be great and what qualities made that athlete so great.
	Extension	Students will create a Venn diagram comparing and contrasting Michael Jordan to the athlete his or her parents chose.
Taking Informed Action (Enrichment)	Students will write to their favorite athlete or artist in order to determine whether they were simply blessed with natural talent or gained success through hard work and passion.	

STAGING THE LESSON

This lesson can be introduced in different ways depending on teaching style and population. The initial goal is to get students to contemplate innate ability and acquired ability through effort. The discussion of what makes us great should move to an evaluation of natural talents an individual is born with or the efforts that the individual makes in pursuit of excellence? This should stimulate a discussion because there will more than likely be a pretty even amount of students on each side of the argument.

It is important to steer the conversation in a way that allows all of your students to see the other points of view in the room. If there is a heavy majority taking a stand on one side, try to foster a debate in the room by supporting the other side. The important thing is to get students to understand the difference between natural ability and acquired ability from our effort. It is permissible if some students say both play a role, which is probably true.

Ultimately, the goal of the lesson is to inspire students to see that they have a fighting chance at something that they may have assumed they were terrible at. If you can get students to truly believe that success is more a result of effort than ability, then they will be willing to work even when the going gets tough.

Here is one way to get the conversation flowing. Without any preface, write the question "What makes people great?" on the board. This is a very general question, which can often be a good thing, because there is really no wrong answer. Students can take this down many different avenues and you can bounce off the answers that bring you to your point. You may get answers like "hard work," "mastery," "success," or "practice."

These are all great starting points. If volunteers are hard to come by, the teacher may have to be a little more specific. Pose a specific example such as, "What made Albert Einstein a great scientist?" (This is a good time to relate to your students, pick an example that would be of interest, especially to those who normally enjoy tuning out.)

Once students are asked a more specific question such as the Albert Einstein example, surely they tend to come up with things such as "he was a genius," "he studied a lot," or "he was determined." It is true he was a genius, but students will be amazed to learn that Einstein really did not do well early in school. Students will be shocked to learn that Einstein nearly dropped out and teacher rarely took him seriously. Einstein only truly fostered his ingenuity later in life when he discovered his *love* (passion) for physics and mathematics.

This is a good place to ask if Albert Einstein was a born genius. Many of students will say yes and for now, it is natural for them to feel that way. Do not try to change their minds. Once the teacher feels your class has had a healthy debate and their neurons are firing away, the students are ready for the case study found in your teacher resources section at the end of the chapter.

Teachers can either make copies for each student or just read the story aloud. Ask the students to keep in mind all of the points they and their classmates just made and then read the case study about Carlos Rodriguez. After the story is completed, have students work in groups or pairs to answer the discussion questions.

The questions are designed to make students think about the series of events that bring Carlos to recognize the effort put in and has earned a place on the school team. In the beginning, Carlos was cocky and boastful, not even willing to practice with friends. By the end of the case study, Carlos realizes that in order to be truly great at soccer it is necessary to practice like everyone else.

Only after his hard work did Carlos make the school team. At this point, it is clear that effort and passion for a goal play a key role in one's success. Not all of students will be fully convinced just yet, but fear not, the lesson has a long way to go!

Natural ability is so constantly praised and admired that students are programmed to think individuals possess a maximum potential level for many activities and skills. When students have completed this staging, they are ready to be introduced to the story. It is hoped that the story and the questions that support the story will have students begin to either question existing beliefs or confirm existing beliefs brought to light in the staging.

THE READ-ALOUD: STORIES THAT STICK

The students are now ready to engage in the read-aloud exploring the story in whatever format that the teacher shares to read the story. Questions before, during, and after the reading are on the template and are provided merely as suggestions.

It is the belief of the authors that questions used to drive the reading are best created by the individual classroom teacher as part of the teachable moments that make read-aloud experiences come to life. More than likely, the suggestions will get you started and follow-up questions will arise in response to students' reactions.

SUMMATIVE PERFORMANCE TASKS

The concluding part of this lesson calls for a short YouTube video about Michael Jordan's devastation upon being cut from his high school basketball team and the actions he then took (https://www.youtube.com/watch?v=aHfUTVDkIIM). The take-away from this video is that Michael did not give up after being cut, but he actually worked twice as hard and made the team when he tried out again the following year. Here is a good time to get another student-led, yet controlled, discussion going among the whole class.

The class may also benefit from coming up with personal examples of natural versus learned ability indicators. This will get them to see the theory as a separate idea from the story. Have students individually fill out the T-chart on "Natural Ability" or "Learned Ability" found in the teacher resources section at the end of this chapter. Here students will be able to come up with terms and phrases that imply either "Natural Ability" or "Learned Ability." Then have students share thoughts with the person sitting next to them to double their responses.

The home assignment is a great way to get students rehash this idea later at home, imprinting it even more into their brains while offering an opportunity to communicate with parents!

Once students retell the story, parent(s) will pick an athlete considered to be great and tell the child what made the athlete of choice so great. For an extension, students will compare and contrast Michael Jordan to the athlete their parents chose. Hopefully, a few similarities emerge and initiate your students to experience mini-brain pops at home and really get the students to believe in this concept that effort and passion make us great.

For enrichment purposes, students can take this a step further. At this point, they know the difference between natural ability and learned ability. They also know that even if they have some natural talent, effort and passion are the driving forces behind greatness.

Students can take all of this knowledge and come up with their own story that demonstrates how one truly becomes great. If this is something you would like your whole class to do, but have students that are not all thrilled about having to be creative, there is another approach. Simply have students research a list of other famous people and evaluate the effect that passion for the goal, effort, and perseverance played in the individual's success.

TAKING INFORMED ACTION

Without real-life application of this theory, the lesson's power fades over time. Therefore in order to keep this theory fresh in students' mindsets, teachers can simply extend the common practice of goal setting. In other words, when asking students to, say, list three short-term goals, not only will they have to state the goals and their means to achieving those goals, but here they should also apply this newfound theory.

In addition to normal goal setting students will be required to list natural abilities as well as learned abilities that will bring them to their desired outcome. This will get students to think about how both natural ability and effort play a role in their success. An example worksheet is provided in the teacher resources section.

This is just one way that teachers can ensure that this theory is applied beyond one day's lesson. Another way is to have students connect to the real world by writing to paragons of grit to learn firsthand the story of what made this person persevere through all hardship and challenge. These connections will make the learning last long after the lesson.

TEACHER RESOURCES

CASE STUDY: CARLOS RODRIGUEZ
The Story:
A fifth grader at the Jefferson Street School, Carlos Rodríguez loved to play soccer more than anything and he knew he was great at it. Everyone at school often complimented Carlos on his natural skill. "You're a natural!" they would say, as he effortlessly kicked the ball into the goal. He often dreamed about becoming a professional soccer player like Lionel Messi when he grew up. Tryouts were only a week away, and all of Carlos's friends were practicing after school every day instead of meeting at the park to play like they usually did. One day that week, Carlos's best friend Jorge asked him why he wasn't practicing with them to prepare for tryouts. Carlos replied, "Psh, I don't need to practice, I'm a natural just like Messi." After tryouts the following week, Carlos went home confident that he would lead the Jefferson Bulldogs to many victories. When the roster was posted at lunch the next day, Carlos was shocked when he could not locate his name on the list. As soon as he arrived home, he threw his soccer ball in the far back corner of his closet and slammed the door.

Figure 10.1.   Case Study: Carlos Rodriguez

When his dad came home from work, he saw Carlos watching TV instead of playing soccer outside like usual, so he asked him why he wasn't practicing. Carlos mumbled, "I'm no good at it anyways. I hate that dumb sport!" Carlos felt like a failure inside, but his dad knew otherwise. His dad then began to tell him about how his favorite famous soccer player, Lionel Messi, was cut from his soccer team when he was Carlos's age. His dad explained, "He didn't give up on himself. He knew that with more practice, he could get better and he could make it. And then, he did!" This story really got Carlos thinking. Messi's story sounded a lot like his! Maybe if he practiced and worked really hard, he could make the team next year and even make it all the way to the World Cup! For the rest of that year, Carlos practiced every single day after school and even on the weekends. When tryouts rolled around the following school year, Carlos was nervous, but confident that this year he was prepared to make the school team. And he did.

Questions:

1) Why didn't Carlos make the team the first time he tried out?
2) Why did Carlos change his mind about giving up soccer?
3) What did Carlos learn after hearing Messi's story?
4) What was different about the second time Carlos tried out for the school's soccer team?

Figure 10.1. Continued

Name: _____   Date:_____

Natural Ability	Learned Ability

Figure 10.2. Natural versus Learned Ability

Chapter 11

Sticking with It

Grit Perseverance for Long-Term Goals

Iggy Peck, Architect by Andrea Beaty and David Roberts

HOW THIS BOOK CONNECTS TO POSITIVE
PSYCHOLOGY RESEARCH ON GRIT

The book *Iggy Peck, Architect* brings to light the difference between grit and perseverance. Perseverance, *sticking with it*, is certainly a key element in grit, but grit, the *passion* for long-term goals and the *perseverance* to overcome obstacles in pursuit of that goal, is often mistaken for being *perseverance* alone. This oversimplified understanding leaves out what may be the key rationale for persevering, *passion for the goal*.

Duckworth's passion for the goal measure is defined in her research by items measuring consistency over time. Grit is not a burning passion that flames in and quickly fades out. Grit is staying the course over time. Duckworth likes to remind us that *grit is living life like it is marathon and not a sprint*.

Where grit intersects with the next section of the book, character strengths, is that grit naturally originates from our strengths, what life calls us to do and what we are passionate about. What enables us to maintain passion for a goal over time is both an affinity for a goal and a character strength that resonates deep within our being. This passion is not always as obvious as Iggy's drive toward architecture, but is one that students must discover and nurture.

Although grit has now become the flavor of the month in educational circles, some of the recent applications miss the essence of the research. Weak math students, who struggle over the easiest problems, are exhorted to

93

have more grit. Struggling math students need self-regulation and persever-ance to finish their work, but grit is not just about resilience. Grit can only be realized when the learner develops a passion for the goal, whether that goal is extrinsic or intrinsic.

This incorrect application of the research on grit has made it the latest panacea for all of our educational ills. This was never Duckworth's intent. It is true that students may have to "suck it up" and work hard when the work is not pleasant, but there is more to grit than pain. "Sucking it up" for a test is about self-regulation and certainly necessary. This action becomes "grit" only when the perseverance is derived from passion for a goal.

The goal can be an extrinsic on an A or passing the test or admission to medical school. Those endeavors can certainly fuel perseverance and are sometimes borne of passion for the goal. However, when the goal is an intrinsic goal, fueled by strengths and affinities, the perseverance can become automatic and painless.

At its core, grit is differentiated in that perseverance is driven by *passion for a goal*. Weaker math students most often do not love math, but need discipline to finish the onerous task of homework. Admonishing that student who hates math to *find his or her grit* might not be an accurate application of the research. On the other hand, asking that struggling math student, "How badly do you want to pass math?" may appropriately help find that student *find his or her grit*.

A talented math student, who perseveres over time to answer a challeng-ing and seemingly impossible problem, might better demonstrate grit than a weaker student working at tasks that are a living hell for the student. This is the passion that resonates in *Salt in His Shoes*. The weaker student needs perseverance to endure the struggle, but passion in that case might arise only from how bad the student needs to pass math.

This book provides a slant of grit research that students and educators may not consider. Grit, as the panacea for what ails us in education, has come to be symbolic of effort that is unpleasant and drudgery. Deliberate practice, focused practice to get better, can be equated with grit and may be thought of an unpleasant and dreadful process that must be endured but not enjoyed. *Iggy Peck, Architect* offers a view of grit as arising from our passion in life and deliberate practice, not only not being onerous, but also being joyful.

Albert Einstein once said, "For me, love is a better teacher than duty." This is the case with Iggy Peck, who loves architecture. Despite his teacher, Miss. Greer, who attempts to extinguish that passion in the classroom, Iggy remains true to his affinity and strength. There is a deep message in this story suggest-ing that students need to find out what life is calling them to do, follow those dreams, and *stick with those dreams*. There is an even deeper message for teachers between the lines of this story revealing *how to get students gritty*.

In the end, Iggy's passion for architecture not only saves Ms. Greer, but it transforms the classroom as well. Iggy's passion for architecture is discovered on his second birthday, but not all students are born with such an obvious passion and life direction. Even Duckworth's passion for grit comes later in life after much exploration. Part of the mission of school should be to help students discover the goals that life seems to be calling them to do and nurture their passion for goals. This may be the secret pathway to grit and making deliberate practice painless.

The book's message for teachers may be more than being flexible in accepting student differences, but in transforming classrooms that allow for students to discover and create their own dreams. Teachers may use the story to inject the power of autonomy and self-direction into their instruction.

Daniel Pink in his award-winning book, *Drive*, shares the research of that what motivates people are not the carrots and sticks of rewards and punishment, but autonomy (self-direction), mastery, and purpose. Ms. Greer transforms her classroom on Fridays, and there is a hope that the book might serve as an inspiration for many teachers to follow that example and transform their classroom.

The book *Learn Like a Pirate* is another great resource for teachers looking to transform their classroom through student ownership of the educational directions. The book urges teachers to have their students collaborate, lead, and succeed. Practical ideas and examples are presented for injecting choice and ownership into instruction.

Finally, Google's *Genius Hour* is an avenue worth investigating. This paradigm shift for teachers provides time in the school day for students to pursue their own passions on projects of their choosing. Again, the story can be the springboard for student discussions on their own strengths and for the institution of a class Genius Hour. This story is a natural lead-in to the idea of strengths covered in the next section of the book.

More detailed information on grit research is available for teachers and parents in the reference section in Chapter 20 of this book. These shared sources on grit include YouTube presentations, life-altering books applying the research to daily life, and a snapshot of the scholarly research from which the positive psychology supporting the chapter has been derived. Teachers are encouraged to dig deeper into developing a rich understanding of the research in order to strengthen the power and delivery of the lesson.

Lesson Design: *Iggy Peck, Architect*
Monica Zenyuh

Table 11.1.   Grit Perseverance for Long-Term Goals: *Iggy Peck, Architect* by Andrea Beaty and David Roberts

Compelling Question	What is passion for a goal and where does it come from?	
Common Core Standards	• CCSS.ELA-LITERACY.CCRA.R.2 • CCSS.ELA-LITERACY.CCRA.SL.1 • CCSS.ELA-LITERACY.CCRA.W.1 • NCSS—Theme 4: Individual Development and Identity • NCSS Inquiry Arc—Dimension 4	
Staging the Question	Students will be given a scrambled word assignment for homework the night before (Teacher Resources 1) to serve as a springboard to the lesson. Sharing answers to this assignment will serve as an opening to this lesson.	

Supporting Question 1 *(Before reading)* What does it mean to be passionate about a goal?	Supporting Question 2 *(During reading)* What is Iggy's passion in Iggy Peck, Architect, and how does Iggy respond when that passion is challenged?	Supporting Question 3 *(After reading)* What role does passion for a goal play in sticking to a goal despite obstacles?
What does it mean to persevere? Why do people continue to work at something even though they face challenges and obstacles? What does it mean to be passionate about something? Are any of you passionate about something? What?	What are the two reactions Iggy's mom has to his design? How does Iggy respond? Why does Ms. Greer prohibit building? What impact does Ms. Greer have on Iggy? How does the collapse of the footbridge change the story?	How did Ms. Greer's opinions change? Did Iggy exhibit perseverance? How? Why did he continue even when people were against him? Why do some people give up their passion? Does Iggy's story remind you of a person you know or have heard about?
Formative Performance Task	*Formative Performance Task*	*Formative Performance Task*
Students will be given an assignment for homework the night before the lesson that will be used to open the lesson.	Students respond to the above questions at key points during the read-aloud of the text.	Students will sort the qualities of failing well from the diagram as presented in Diagram 2 in a format chosen by the teacher.
Featured Sources	*Featured Sources*	*Featured Sources*
Teacher Resource #1.	*Iggy Peck, Architect* by Andrea Beaty and David Roberts	Teacher Resources #2 and 3.

Summative Performance Tasks	Design Challenge Extension	Students will work in cooperative groups to complete a design challenge (Teacher Resource #3).

	Writing Extension	Students will retell the story to their parents. They will write a short paragraph detailing a personal story from their parents' life and their own life where they exhibited perseverance borne of passion (Teacher Resource #2).
Taking Informed Action (Enrichment)		Students will share the story of their parents exhibiting perseverance and create a class bulletin board containing a one-sentence Post-it summary from their personal story (Perseverance Postings). Students will create a Genius Hour experience in their own classrooms.

STAGING THE LESSON

This lesson contains an introductory and concluding activity that may be performed in the reverse order, if the teacher wishes. The goal is to both begin and end the lesson with activities that make the students think about what qualities are involved in trying to accomplish goals (both short- and long-term). Both activities involve grit and perseverance, and for some activities, they incorporate *a passion for the goal.*

It is suggested that this lesson begin with students taking out their homework from the night before. Students were challenged to unscramble two different words (*cooperation* and *perseverance*) with the assistance of an adult and to answer several questions as they did so.

Students were asked to time themselves unscrambling both for three reasons that can be shared the day after they complete the activity: (1) to see if the amount of time spent on the activity influenced if students stuck with it or stopped; (2) to see how long students persevered in the activity; (3) to provide a little external pressure, which often accompanies challenges. As the teacher circulates around the room to check on the words and time spent, he or she will gain preliminary information on the time students invested and on the level of success.

This activity envisions the teacher asking for students to indicate the number of words solved correctly: 1 finger for the first word, 2 fingers for the second word, and their full hand for both words. After the show of hands, the teacher should elicit the two words formed and then discuss why the students think that the teacher chose these two words (there's always an ulterior motive!), which will lead to a conversation about what perseverance is.

Some questions that can trigger conversation include, What does it mean to persevere? Why do people continue to work at something even though they face challenges and obstacles? What are some examples of people you've heard of that have persevered over obstacles to achieve a goal? What have you persevered in? This conversation will hopefully lead to a discussion on the idea of how badly you want to achieve a goal introducing the idea of passion for a goal.

THE READ-ALOUD: STORIES THAT STICK

The students are now ready to engage in the read-aloud exploring the story in whatever format that the teacher shares to read the story. The students are now ready for the book, and subsequent activities and challenges will bring the story to life. The teacher will not explain the nature of the book, but will have the students make personal connections during, after, and *long after* the reading.

Some questions for before, during, and after the reading are on the template and are provided merely as suggestions. It is the belief of the authors that questions used to drive the reading are best created by the individual classroom teacher as part of the teachable moments that make read-aloud experiences come to life. The suggestions on the template might be used to get the lesson started, and follow-up questions should naturally arise in response to students' reactions.

SUMMATIVE PERFORMANCE TASK

This story will be followed up in two ways in order to experience these terms and apply them to situations in their own lives. However, there are many other ways of achieving this than the following ideas. Teachers know best what will work in the room. Tweak these ideas to suit needs, or use the ideas as a springboard to new ideas that developed as a result of the reading this or class's interest.

Reading this book immediately makes one think that a design challenge is in order. Actually, three or four come to mind, but for the sake of time and space, only one will be described in depth here. The point is that many design challenges focus on the process of trial and error and cause students to go back and rethink and redesign and realize that everything cannot be solved instantaneously.

This is a crucial skill to develop in today's society where answers are often readily at one's fingertips. Immersing students in activities that rely on cooperation and perseverance is important to facilitate a classroom environment that promotes risk-taking and where students stop using the word "can't" and find other ways to express and address frustrations.

The design challenge (Teacher Resource #3) that was chosen for this activity involves building a structure (like Iggy) with very limited materials, which helps with time and budgetary constraints. All that is needed is a package of letter-sized cardstock paper (8 ½ x 11 ½) and small (3 oz.) plastic or paper cups (15 needed per group). This activity was designed for students to work in small groups (3 or 4 students) so that they may work cooperatively and share ideas, but this activity can alter based on individual preference and teaching style.

The premise of the activity is that Iggy Peck is purchasing the small island visited on that fateful day. Iggy envisions constructing a small building to serve as another school where the students can work on island visits. Since it is in a flood zone, there is a need for the school to be put up on stilts. Students are given the task of designing a sketch for a small building that is supported by stilts and has at least two floors.

Students are told that they will be focusing only on the floors and supports at this stage of the game, and will be able to use only 5 sheets of paper and 15 small cups. Providing design constraints makes students think toward a common goal, but also forces students to think outside the box, as there are limitations to what one might ordinarily suggest.

Time constraints are given to keep students on task but these, again, may be adjusted as the teacher sees fit. Space is provided for multiple designs, as students must be reminded that the process of designing and building is one of trial and error, and very rarely is the first design the one that is in the final product.

Once the time has expired, extra time should be given for students to observe what other groups have thought of. (It is also recommended that teachers take pictures of the work at these different stages, as these pictures can provide valuable learning experiences later on as students reflect or even if the pictures are just posted on a board for students to look at during free time and think about.)

This lesson then throws in another challenge, with the goal of making students go back to the drawing board, literally and figuratively, to make changes in order to realize success. Models must be tested before designs can be implemented. So, while humans are not able to stand on these floors, the teacher has selected some models that can do this for us.

At this time, the teacher presents small-sized bean-filled animals (using two or three of the same exact ones will provide equity) that students will use to "test" if the building is stable. The teacher then visits each group and asks the group to place one of the models on the structure to see if the structure remains standing. It is expected that most will not.

Students will then flip over the design challenge papers to reveal that there is a space provided to draw a new sketch for how they can construct a building to hold this model. It might be best to give students 10 more minutes to complete this part of the challenge, and then, after the time expires, to take pictures and discuss what did and didn't work.

An extension of this activity is to answer three questions pertaining to the design challenge and Iggy Peck and to focus on the terms that are consistent throughout both of them. Students will be able to begin answering these questions in class if they finished early, but otherwise they will be asked to complete them for homework.

The following day, the class should be asked to share some of the challenges faced and ways that the group overcame them, along with some of the answers to the previous night's questions. The teacher should then collect the design challenges and assessment questions to use in whatever manner that best meets instructional needs.

The follow-up discussion will seek out what role architectural passion and capacity played in perseverance. Were students more likely quit if they did not like or have talent in building and to persevere if they loved the activity? The idea that perseverance is nurtured by passion should emerge from the discussion.

At this point, it is recommended that the teacher bring everything full circle and tie in with the word scramble, the story, and the design challenge to reinforce the concept of perseverance and how it ties in with passion and grit. It is hoped that these three activities will blend in seamlessly and create some "Ah-Ha!" moments that cause lightbulbs to light. Adding in the following extension will provide a connection to home and more real-world applications of the concepts at the heart of this lesson and is strongly recommended.

Extension

To extend the book and concepts to the real world for homework, students will be asked to go home and share the story by summarizing *Iggy Peck, Architect* with an adult. Students will then be required to ask this adult about a time he or she exhibited perseverance to achieve something they were passionate about.

The students will then share a story with this adult. To conclude, they will summarize each story in five to seven sentences on the worksheet provided to bring to class to share the next day. Sharing the read-aloud story and then personal stories will provide for different perspectives on perseverance and allow for more in-depth class discussions on ways people handle obstacles in life.

TAKING INFORMED ACTION

Sharing all of the stories of the students and their parents may prove to be a challenge, yet only allowing a few to share may not sit well with others. A solution to this problem is to create a bulletin board with a catchy title

(Perseverance Postings or Posting Perseverance) whereby each student receives a large Post-it to write one sentence that summarizes one of the events shared in the homework assignment.

Writing this one sentence about a personal example of perseverance provides several educational benefits. First, summarizing and writing succinctly are key goals of the CCSS, and recognizing and noting the main idea of their story accomplishes this. Second, getting to the heart of perseverance and motivation and grit and getting students to think about what they are passionate about are life skills that have been proven to have strong correlations with success in life.

Finally students will ask how they might transform their classroom the way that Miss Greer did on Fridays. At this point, through the website Genioushour.com students will lay the groundwork for constructing their own Genius Hour in the spirit of Miss Greer. It is encouraged that students watch the RSA video on motivation (drive) in order to know the power of discovering and unleashing their passion.

TEACHER RESOURCES

Teacher Direction Sheets

Name: _____ Date: _____

Word Scramble

Activity Description: One of our lessons in class tomorrow will depend on this assignment. Your job is to follow the directions below as you time how long it takes you to unscramble two words (one in each baggie) with an adult in your household.

Directions:

1. Open bag #1 and place all of the cards in front of both of you with the letters facing up. When you are set, begin your timer (or look at your clock for a start time) and move the letters around to use **all** of the letters to spell **one** word. When you figure out the word, enter the time it took you to create it and then answer the questions below. (If you need more room to write, you may continue on the back.)

   Word created: _____

   Amount of Time: _____

2. What problems/setbacks did you face as you worked?

_____

_____

_____

_____

3. Did you use any strategies that helped you? _____

_____

_____

_____

_____

4. Put those letters back in baggie #1. Then open up baggie #2 and put the letters in front of you like you did before. Begin your timer and try to figure out this word together.

   Word created: _____

   Amount of Time: _____

5. Was it harder or easier to create this word? Why? _____

_____

_____

_____

_____

6. Together, discuss what this word means, and write down a definition that you came up with in your own words on the lines below.

_____

_____

CULMINATING REFLECTIONS

Name: _____   Date: _____

Directions: Summarize the story *Iggy Peck, Architect* for an adult in your home. Then, think about a time when each of you exhibited perseverance in life about something that you were passionate about and share it with each other. On the lines below, write a short summary of what you shared including the setbacks you experienced, and why you wanted to continue on despite experiencing these setbacks (approximately 5–7 sentences each).

Iggy Peck, Architect Design Challenge

Scenario: Iggy just purchased the small island to construct a small building for his class. Since it is in a flood zone, it will need to be built on *stilts*. He has asked you to create a preliminary sketch and a small model to give him some more ideas. You are only required to show the floors and supports (no walls or a roof, yet). The building must be freestanding and have a minimum of two floors. You will be given 15 minutes to design and then build the structure you designed using ONLY the following materials that you will be given to work with:

*5 sheets of cardstock paper   (floors) *15 small (3 oz.) cups (stilts and supports)

Step 1: Design—In **pencil**, draw a sketch of how you intend to build your building in box A. Once you finish your design plan, show it to the teacher to receive your materials.

Step 2: Construction—Now that you have your materials, build what you designed above in box A.

Step 3: Test—Does your building stand on its own without assistance? If yes, call over the teacher to see it. If no, go back to the drawing board. Go up to box B and draw a new design. Once this is completed, build it! (If a third design is needed, you may draw it in the space below.)

**When the bell sounds, stop working, as the time is up!

Step 4: Design Challenge—Since this is just a model, we won't test your building's strength with a person. Instead we will use a model that the teacher will give you to represent a person. Place this model on the top floor of your building. Did it remain standing? If not, a new design must be constructed. Draw this in box **C**.

Step 4: Design Test—When your new plan is created, get your model from the teacher and test it. If it did not remain standing, draw one final design in box D (above).

Step 5: Analysis and Drawing Conclusions—Write the following questions down on a piece of loose leaf. Once you have written down all three, you may begin forming your own individual responses. If you do not have time to complete this in class, you will be asked to finish this for homework tonight so that you are ready for our class discussion tomorrow. Every member of your group's answers will be stapled to this design challenge and then collected by the teacher.

On Your Own Questions:

1. What were some challenges that you and your group encountered during this activity? How did you try to overcome these?
2. Does perseverance always lead to success? Why or why not?
3. Does having a passion for something affect how hard someone will work toward a future goal in this area? (For example: If one person really cared about creating a building that worked and another person didn't, could that affect the outcome?)

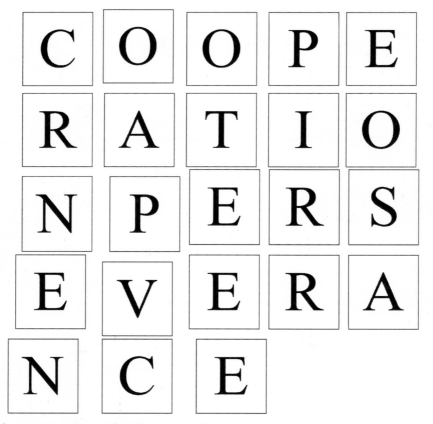

Figure 11.1.   Cooperation Perseverance Letters

A:	B:
C:	D:

Figure 11.2.   Iggy Peck Design Templates

Chapter 12

Sustaining Grit

The Power of Passion for a Goal

No You Can't, Yes I Can by Justin Allen and Antoinette Cauley

---

HOW THIS BOOK CONNECTS TO POSITIVE
PSYCHOLOGY RESEARCH ON GRIT

In her recent conversations with Pete Carroll of the Seattle Seahawks, Angela Duckworth profiles paragons of grit and identifies three distinct stages that define truly gritty people. The first of those stages involves a fascination and passion for the activity or subject. Most people can summon up a time when the infatuation with an idea or an activity took over their lives.

As discussed in the previous books, what distinguishes the *gritty people* from others is that *they* follow that initial passion with a prolonged specific and deliberate practice that is more involved than just working at something as one does in a sport practice. Duckworth elaborates *on deliberate practice as practice in pursuit of a stretch goal, focusing on the specific improvement of weaknesses with specific feedback on what needs to be done to improve.*

Passion for the goal might be what enables one to endure deliberate practice over time. The story of Justin Allen presented in *No You Can't, Yes I Can* reveals the power of persistence over time borne of Justin's extreme passion for the game of basketball.

At every stage of life in confronting challenge, Justin is told that he can't, but extreme passion enables Justin to overcome all doubters. What is not in the text, but needs to be made clear to students, is that Justin endured long hours of deliberate practice to achieve his success. Many students become infatuated with an activity at early ages, but only those with genuine passion for the goal will pursue a serious enough deliberate practice routine to achieve the goals in the face of stressors.

To highlight the difference between deliberate practice and regular practice, Duckworth shares personal insights on the fact that despite her own daily running, there is a lack of improvement in her running times. For improvement to happen, Duckworth would need to seek out specific feedback, run certain lengths with prescribed times in attempt to address running deficiencies, seriously weight train, and focus intently on putting in the time needed over time to achieve the desired improvement in race time.

Duckworth would need deliberate practice, but the goal of running is not driven by a true passion for lower times, but merely by enjoyment of running. With this example in mind, students can reflect on their own deliberate practices in regard to schoolwork. Those who are more passionate about grades or a goal in life to be achieved tend to exhibit more of the deliberate practice needed to get to that goal.

In life, it is not uncommon to encounter students with tremendous academic capacity but little passion for achieving an education, and, conversely, those with less capacity possessed unbelievable work efforts. There is little doubt who fares better. Effort trumps ability. At this point, students might begin to recognize the positive psychology of growth mindset, hope, and grit as interdependent and correlated.

To clarify the role of effort and grit, Duckworth provides two mathematical equations in her book *Grit: Passion and Perseverance for Long Term Goals* to have students understand the role of effort or practice in pursuit of a goal. The first equation suggests that talent times effort equals skill, and in that equation effort counts twice. The second equation proposes that skill times effort equals achievement. Again, in this formula, effort counts twice. These equations are powerful insights that may not be fully appreciated by students until years in the future.

Duckworth's final stage in the life of gritty individuals is purpose. Those who endure the deliberate practice to develop grit in pursuit of achievement generally move to a higher purpose than just individual achievement. At the heart of their grit is a belief that what the individual does matters to others and this sense of purpose is a driving force in their lives.

All three of the factors Duckworth suggests are characteristic of paragons of grit that are brought to life in *No You Can't, Yes I Can*. Justin is possessed by an initial passion for the game of basketball that enables the deliberate practice necessary to overcome stressors that would have wilted the passion of others. In doing so, the book provides an answer to the question of the compelling question: *Does the passion for a goal create the perseverance for that goal?*

Through the sharing of the story, students should discover that the author's goal is more than to share personal greatness in basketball. The true purpose to Justin's struggle is imparting that the power of passion for a goal arms an individual with a perseverance that can overcome any obstacle.

More detailed information on grit research is available for teachers and parents in the reference section in Chapter 20 of this book. These shared sources on grit include YouTube presentations, life-altering books applying the research to daily life, and a snapshot of the scholarly research from which the positive psychology supporting the chapter has been derived. Teachers are encouraged to dig deeper into developing a rich understanding of the research in order to strengthen the power and delivery of the lesson.

Lesson Design: *No You Can't, Yes I Can*
Dan Keegan and Jessica Keegan

Table 12.1.   The Power of Passion for a Goal: *No You Can't, Yes I Can* by Justin Allen and Antoinette Cauley

Compelling Question	Does passion for a goal create perseverance for that goal?
Common Core Standards	• CCSS.ELA-LITERACY.CCRA.R.2 • CCSS.ELA-LITERACY.CCRA.SL.1 • CCSS.ELA-LITERACY.CCRA.W.1 • NCSS—Theme 4: Individual Development and Identity • NCSS Inquiry Arc—Dimension 4
Staging the Question	https://www.youtube.com/watch?v=GyJJ1XnNy0U *A Lesson in Perseverance: Award Winning Author Shares Personal Struggle to Write.* After viewing the video clip on Kate DiCamillo's writing career, ask students to define perseverance. Working in pairs, students should discuss an event in their lives when they were rejected or turned down. It will be important to review strategies used to overcome these struggles. These three stages will be reinforced through the supporting questions.

Supporting Question 1 (Before reading) What does passion for a goal in your life look like?	*Supporting Question 2 (During reading)* What enables Justin Allen in No You Can't, Yes I Can to achieve his goals in the face of those who challenge his ability to overcome his problems and shortcomings?	*Supporting Question 3 (After reading)* What is the relationship of passion for a goal and one's ability to persevere through stressors and obstacles?
What does passion look like, sound like, and feel like in your life? How do you define passion for a goal? How does your passion for a goal make you behave?	What qualities or character traits help individuals persevere in the face of challenges and obstacles?	Can passion lead an individual to persevere in the face of challenges?

Continued

Table 12.1.   Continued

Formative Performance Task	Formative Performance Task	Formative Performance Task
Students will sketch a picture of themselves pursuing a passion. This picture should show something they have strong emotions about. Students will then share in a forum. The passions will be charted in the first column of a 3-column chart to show examples of the kinds of things that inspire strong emotion or love.	While reading *No You Can't, Yes I Can*, students should create a chart highlighting challenges faced by Justin Allen and the qualities/traits that helped Mr. Allen persevere. A fourth column may be added to examine whether these qualities/traits are internal (belief in self) or external (strengthen skills).	Groups will create a 3-column chart containing: • Passions • Stressors • Behaviors of perseverance Students should highlight rows where behaviors of perseverance could lessen the power of the stressor on the passion.
Featured Sources	Featured Sources	Featured Sources
https://www.youtube.com/watch?v=GyJJ1XnNy0U https://www.youtube.com/watch?v=UNAMrZr9O WYhttps://www.youtube.com/watch?v=UNAMrZr9OWY	*No You Can't, Yes I Can!* by Justin Allen and Antoinette Cauley Perseverance Chart	See Lesson Plan for suggested websites

Summative Performance Task	Argument	Does passion inspire perseverance? Students will work collaboratively to create a reflective piece to show a passion, a stressor, or a challenge that threatens the passion, and a behavior that fuels perseverance in pursuit of the passion. Students can produce a skit, a video, a storyboard, a cartoon, or a written script.
	Extension	Students will retell *No You Can't, Yes I Can!* as well as their own story to their family and elicit from them a time someone in their family persevered in pursuit of a passion. Students will draw a picture or share a story creating their own *No You Can't, Yes We Can* class book.
Taking Informed Action (Enrichment)		As a means to harness student learning and growth, while also bringing their newfound knowledge and skills to the world, students will look to the news and current events locally or nationally to identify children or families facing challenges. Students will write letters to these individuals and/or families, care of the newspaper, to show both understanding and respect for the level of perseverance it takes to overcome stressors and challenges, as well as to encourage and support perseverance.

Table 12.2. Your Personal Perseverance Chart Examples

Passion	Stressor/Challenges	Persevering Behaviors (Deliberate Practice Needed)
Basketball	Height	Belief in self and knowing you can play
		Hours of work on weaknesses
		Coaching and clinics
Guitar	Finding time for practice	Making practice a priority by playing first thing in the morning
		Great instruction
		Practicing pieces that are difficult

STAGING THE LESSON

Students may have a vague understanding of perseverance. It's a word that is invoked at times of stress or need, but to examine situations of perseverance when not under stress will be valuable in building the kind of behaviors that will help a child persevere. Students will watch a video of award-winning author Kate DiCamillo, with whom many will be familiar. DiCamillo's success will be something students can understand and may have witnessed in many of her award-winning novels.

Students will see that DiCamillo was not always successful in having books published. There are startling images of the many rejection folders organized by DiCamillo. This visual of the stressors of rejection by her publishers should be relatable to other stressors. Students will then be asked to work in pairs to brainstorm other people/places that stress on a passion can come from. Students may talk about parents, friends, grandparents, teachers, instructors, or themselves.

The suggested activity accompanying supporting question 3 involves a multistep process for peer-to-peer and whole-class collaboration.

1. Each student should be given time to begin the 3-column chart, listing one to three things that they are passionate about.
2. After completing the 3-column chart, the student should meet with a group of three or four partners to review their groups' passions, stressors/challenges, and potential persevering behaviors and deliberate practice needed. (Students should be encouraged to complete the chart for their classmates' passions, thereby acknowledging and validating the passions of others, while also committing to help these classmates persevere and rise above the stressors and challenges that stand in the way.)
3. Once each student in the small group has had time to share personal passions, stressors/challenges, and potential persevering behaviors, a whole-class review of this activity should commence.

- Though students have had the opportunity to work with a small group, it will be helpful for each student to share with the class one passion, stressors/challenges that may stand in the way, and potential persevering behaviors that may lead to the fulfillment of this passion.
- Additional classmates should be given the opportunity to share additional ways a student may persevere or overcome the stressors and challenges.
- A completed chart will include multiple ways in which a student may be able to persevere through stressors and challenges.

THE READ-ALOUD: STORIES THAT STICK

The students are now ready to engage in the read-aloud exploring the story in whatever format that the teacher chooses to share the story. Questions before, during, and after the reading are on the template and are provided merely as suggestions.

It is the belief of the authors that questions used to drive the reading are best created by the individual classroom teacher as part of the teachable moments that make read-aloud experiences come to life. More than likely, the suggestions will get you started and follow-up questions will arise in response to students' reactions.

Table 12.3. Textual Evidence: Justin Allen's Perseverance Chart

Challenge	Qualities/ Traits That Enable Justin to Overcome Stressors	Evidence from Text "The Voice in Justin's Head"	Internal/ External
Too small for basketball	Passion for the game	"Big or small, I know I can ball"	Internal
From a small town	Driven to perfect his technique	"Your doubts only drive me to perfect my technique"	External
Doubters	Inspirational goals	"Fear is not something that will stand in my way"	Internal
Cancer	Confidence and upbeat attitude	"With love, passion, and drive, I will beat cancer, I will survive."	Internal
Told he can't play after cancer	Willpower	"I will not quit and I will not stop trying"	Internal
Body is beaten up/injuries	Fire still burns	"But my fire still burns and I won't turn back"	Internal
Lack of belief in his writing ability	Belief in self	"I shared it from my heart and from deep within. All of struggle, yet few of dare."	Internal

SUMMATIVE PERFORMANCE TASKS

Argument

Students will work alone or collaboratively with others with a common interest or theme to create a reflective piece to show a passion, a stressor, or a challenge that threatens the passion, and a behavior that fuels perseverance in pursuit of the passion. Students will then share the deliberate practice that will be needed to overcome the stressor.

Students can produce a skit, a video, a storyboard, a hallway display, a video project (documentary), a class presentation to another grade level in the school, a cartoon, or a written script to share with others that may be struggling with a similar stressor/challenge or to fuel a similar passion.

These presentations should be centered on the theme of *Perseverance in the Face of Obstacles*. These presentations should give students the chance to:

- State their passions
- Acknowledge the stressors/challenges that they will face
- Outline the "game plan" and "deliberate practice" needed for persevering

In all live or recorded presentation modes, it is suggested that students dress in a way that relates to their passion. A student who dreams of becoming a surgeon should be encouraged to present/be recorded while wearing hospital scrubs.

This segment may also provide the opportunity for a meaningful research task. While following the same presentation ideas as earlier, a teacher may want to introduce historical examples of people who achieved great success only after failure. These historical examples may be part of the classroom display/presentation.

A few resources to support this research component are as follows:

- http://www.businessinsider.com/successful-people-who-failed-at-first-2015–7
- https://www.wanderlustworker.com/12-famous-people-who-failed-before-succeeding/
- http://www.creativitypost.com/psychology/famous_failures
- http://www.onlinecollege.org/2010/02/16/50-famously-successful-people-who-failed-at-first/

Extension

Students will retell *No You Can't, Yes I Can!* as well as their own story to their family and elicit from them a time someone in their family persevered in pursuit of a passion. Students should create a section of their own class book,

No You Can't, Yes We Can, highlighting their family's personal perseverance story, complete with illustration.

TAKING INFORMED ACTION

As a means to harness student learning and growth while also bringing their newfound knowledge and skills to the world, students will look to the news and current events locally or nationally to identify children or families with either a passion or facing a challenge or both. Students will write letters to these individuals or families (care of the newspaper) to show both understanding and respect for the level of perseverance it takes to overcome stressors and challenges, as well as to encourage and support behaviors of perseverance.

Students will write letters to these individuals to:

- Introduce themselves
- Show understanding of the individual and/or family's passion or challenge/ stressor
- Encourage behaviors of perseverance

Some examples of individuals and/or families students might identify are as follows:

- http://www.usatoday.com/story/news/nation/2013/11/15/batkid-san-fran cisco/3588173/
- http://www.newsday.com/long-island/suffolk/children-with-dis abilities-have-new-playground-in-west-sayville-1.11028839
- http://longisland.news12.com/news/dozens-displaced-when-fire-rips-through-ocean side-building-on-long-beach-road-1.11727278
- http://www.newsday.com/long-island/nassau/etched-in-sand-in spires-glen-head-teen-s-foster-kid-event-1.11642578

Name: _____   Date:_____

In school we have been studying a character whose passion was often thwarted by negative forces. He used techniques like positive thought to help himself persevere.

My team and I created a _____ to show another story of how passion can be supported by positivity.

Can you tell me about a time you had a passion, and something or someone got in the way, and yet you persevered? (Student will write or draw about a family member's story below.)

Section II D: Unlocking Strengths: Discovering and Nurturing Natural Talents

Chapter 13

Spotting Strengths

Strength Finding

Giraffes Can't Dance by Giles Andreae and Guy Parker-Rees

HOW THIS BOOK CONNECTS TO POSITIVE PSYCHOLOGY RESEARCH ON CHARACTER STRENGTHS

Giraffes Can't Dance imparts the understanding that each individual possesses character strengths and that these strengths not only uniquely define that individual but also provide a pathway to success for that individual. Ultimately, it is the individual's strengths that will define the course and direction of one's life.

The start of the story finds Gerald the giraffe believing that he has no special talent and only a weakness for dancing. With the help of a cricket, Gerald discovers his strengths and how to harness these strengths to become the best dancer in the forest. This allegorical story is a perfect introduction into the idea of character strengths. There are far too many Geralds in classrooms across America and around the world.

Tom Rath, in the book *StrengthsFinder 2.0*, introduced the world to the ideas of his grandfather, Donald O. Clifton, who had spent a lifetime of research characterizing strengths and leading millions to discover personal strengths. Clifton's work resulted in the Clifton Strength Finder. This instrument and research emphasized the fact that life is better driven by what individuals do to harness strengths than how successfully individuals overcome and address weaknesses.

Chris Peterson and Martin Seligman in their book *Character Strengths and Virtues: A Handbook and Classification* brought the idea of strengths and virtues to entirely new levels by identifying a classification of six virtues and twenty-four character strengths. Their character traits assessment is offered for free online on the VIA Institute's website: www.viacharacter.org. Figure 13.1 classifies the families of identified strengths and virtues.

The work of David Yeager, Shari Fisher, and David Shearon, graduates of the University of Pennsylvania's Master in Applied Positive Psychology Program, has provided an extraordinary tool for educators with their book and training program on how to teach students to harness their strengths. Their book *SMART Strengths*, from which the Strength 360 Activity in this lesson is

The VIA Classification of 24 Character Strengths

VIA INSTITUTE ON CHARACTER   ViaCharacter.org

WISDOM	**CREATIVITY** • Originality • Adaptive • Ingenuity	**CURIOSITY** • Interest • Novelty-Seeking • Exploration • Openness	**JUDGMENT** • Critical Thinking • Thinking Things Through • Open-mindedness	**LOVE OF LEARNING** • Mastering New Skills & Topics • Systematically Adding to Knowledge	**PERSPECTIVE** • Wisdom • Providing Wise Counsel • Taking the Big Picture View
COURAGE	**BRAVERY** • Valor • Not Shrinking from Fear • Speaking Up for What's Right	**PERSEVERANCE** • Persistence • Industry • Finishing What One Starts	**HONESTY** • Authenticity • Integrity	**ZEST** • Vitality • Enthusiasm • Vigor • Energy • Feeling Alive	
HUMANITY	**LOVE** • Both Loving and Being Loved • Valuing Close Relations with Others	**KINDNESS** • Generosity • Nurturance • Care & Compassion • Altruism • "Niceness"			**SOCIAL INTELLIGENCE** • Aware of the Motives/ Feelings of Self/Others • Knowing what Makes Other People Tick
JUSTICE	**TEAMWORK** • Citizenship • Social Responsibility • Loyalty			**FAIRNESS** • Just • Not Letting Feelings Bias Decisions About Others	**LEADERSHIP** • Organizing Group Activities • Encouraging a Group to Get Things Done
TEMPERANCE		**FORGIVENESS** • Mercy • Accepting Others' Shortcomings • Giving People a Second Chance	**HUMILITY** • Modesty • Letting One's Accomplishments Speak for Themselves	**PRUDENCE** • Careful • Cautious • Not Taking Undue Risks	**SELF-REGULATION** • Self-Control • Disciplined • Managing Impulses & Emotions
TRANSCENDENCE	**APPRECIATION OF BEAUTY & EXCELLENCE** • Awe • Wonder • Elevation	**GRATITUDE** • Thankful for the Good • Expressing Thanks • Feeling Blessed	**HOPE** • Optimism • Future-Mindedness • Future Orientation	**HUMOR** • Playfulness • Bringing Smiles to Others • Lighthearted	**SPIRITUALITY** • Religiousness • Faith • Purpose • Meaning

Figure 13.1.   VIA Classification of Strengths

adapted and borrowed, is a hands-on compilation of strategies on how students can best recognize and harness the power of their individual character strengths.

Their acronym, SMART Strengths, is a strength's intervention that the authors have piloted in schools across America to teach and research character strengths. The program seeks to have student *spot* their unique character strengths and the strengths in others, and manage those strengths. The authors urge students to be aware of the dark or shadow side of strengths, which can involve the negative outcomes that can occur when strengths are misapplied. In this case, the strength can actually block the individual's path to success.

The shadow side of humor can become a weakness when inappropriate humor is injected at the wrong times. This self-knowledge is paramount if a student is to *advocate* for their strengths by building bridges to others with their strengths as connectors. Advocating for strengths can lead directly to *relating* the idea of combining strengths in a synergy with others to form a more rounded and effective group that can better harness the strengths of all.

Most powerfully, training others in identifying and using their strengths can bring the understanding and employment of strengths to new levels. When students teach about skills to other students, they can bring to life the old axiom that if you really want to know something, *teach it*. The model for the SMART Strengths Program can be found in Figure 13.2, and more information on the SMART Strengths program training can be found on the website www.smartstrengths.com.

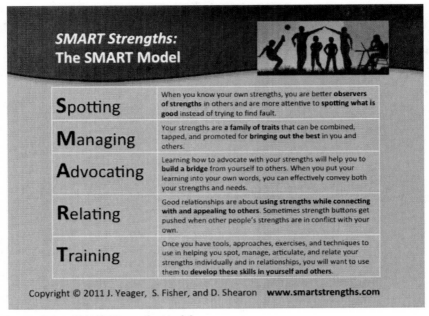

Spotting	When you know your own strengths, you are better **observers of strengths** in others and are more attentive to **spotting what is good** instead of trying to find fault.
Managing	Your strengths are **a family of traits** that can be combined, tapped, and promoted for **bringing out the best** in you and others.
Advocating	Learning how to advocate with your strengths will help you to **build a bridge** from yourself to others. When you put your learning into your own words, you can effectively convey both your strengths and needs.
Relating	Good relationships are about **using strengths while connecting with and appealing to others**. Sometimes strength buttons get pushed when other people's strengths are in conflict with your own.
Training	Once you have tools, approaches, exercises, and techniques to use in helping you spot, manage, articulate, and relate your strengths individually and in relationships, you will want to use them to **develop these skills in yourself and others**.

Copyright © 2011 J. Yeager, S. Fisher, and D. Shearon **www.smartstrengths.com**

Figure 13.2. *SMART* Strengths Model

More detailed information on character strengths research is available for teachers and parents in the reference section in Chapter 20 of this book. These shared sources on character strengths include YouTube presentations, life-altering books applying the research to daily life, and a snapshot of the scholarly research from which the positive psychology supporting the chapter has been derived. Teachers are encouraged to dig deeper into developing a rich understanding of the research in order to strengthen the power and delivery of the lesson.

Lesson Design: *Giraffes Can't Dance*
Amy Kanavy-Curry

Table 13.1.   Strength Finding: *Giraffes Can't Dance* by Giles Andreae and Guy Parker-Rees

Compelling Question	Is it more important to remedy our weaknesses or find our strengths?
Common Core Standards	• CCSS.ELA-LITERACY.CCRA.R.2 • CCSS.ELA-LITERACY.CCRA.SL.1 • CCSS.ELA-LITERACY.CCRA.W.1 • NCSS—Theme 4: Individual Development and Identity • NCSS Inquiry Arc—Dimension 4
Staging the Question	Students will classify character strengths by placing them in order from strongest to weakest. Pose the question, Is it more important to work on your weaknesses or to work on your strengths?

Supporting Question 1 (Before reading) What are more important, our character strengths or our character weaknesses?	Supporting Question 2 (During reading) How does finding and employing his strengths make music that changes life for Gerald the giraffe in Giraffes Can't Dance?	Supporting Question 3 (After reading) What are the strengths that drive your life and make the music in your life?
What are your strengths? What are your weaknesses? Is it more important to work on your strengths or to work on your weaknesses?	Can you identify Gerald the giraffe's weakness? What made dancing difficult for Gerald? Why did Gerald freeze up? How did Gerald learn to dance? What about Gerald's physical nature that helped him discover his song? Did he do it alone? What does "Sometimes when you're different you just need a different song" mean? Can you change the bold words in this statement so it doesn't apply to just dancing: "We all can **dance** when we find **music** that we love?"	At the beginning of the story, does Gerald focus more on his strengths or his weaknesses? Does this work for him? Has there ever been a time where you "froze up" and felt embarrassed you couldn't do something other people could? Gerald was inspired by the moon; can you think of something in your life that inspires you? The end of the book describes Gerald as the best dancer the jungle has ever seen; when do you feel at your best?

Formative Performance Task	Formative Performance Task	Formative Performance Task
The students will view a model dividing a set of eight character strengths and ordering them from strongest to weakest. They will complete the same task and "pair and share" their results. They will provide reasoning for their placement. A class Wordle will be created so the class can view the diversity of their strengths.	Students will work in partnerships to identify the answers to the questions during the read-aloud.	Students will first take a free VIA character strengths test online. After identifying strengths, students will complete an activity called *Strength 360* in which they work with their classmates to determine their strengths. In this activity, unlike the before-reading activity, the students will be recognizing the specific character strengths in their classmates rather than themselves. They will make their selection based on provided words and must offer specific examples to support the words of their choosing. [Source: SMART Strengths]
Featured Sources	*Featured Sources*	*Featured Sources*
The 24 Character Strengths by Chris Peterson and Martin Seligman http://www.wordle.net/create	*Giraffes Can't Dance* by Giles Andreae and Guy Parker-Rees	Find Your Strengths VIA-Virtues in Action

Summative Performance Task	**Argument**	With a carefully selected partner, students will create a Google slideshow that supports how their partner demonstrates two specific character strengths over a consistent period of time. Examples from the person's life should be used, and a variety of sources will be encouraged (parents, classmates, partners). Students will find a successful person who also possessed these traits and explain how they helped them succeed.
	Extension	Students will keep a strengths journal. Any time they feel they are at their best, received a compliment from someone, or notice any unique qualities that seem to set them apart from others, they will jot it down in their strengths journals. Weekly, they will conference with a peer, parent(s), and/or teacher to determine patterns or repetition of a particular skill.

Continued

Table 13.1.   Continued

Taking Informed Action (Enrichment)	Students will include their parents in their investigation of strengths. Their parents will be asked to identify two strengths that they believe their child has based on the provided character strengths and produce specific examples to support the traits chosen. Parents will be encouraged to verbally continue this task as an ongoing reinforcement of identifying a child's strengths as they grow and change.
	Students may become school strength ambassadors by bringing the modified strength lessons to lower grades.

STAGING THE LESSON

Students will be asked, "Is the secret to life discovering your strengths or working diligently on your weaknesses?" Students should be given ample time to internalize this, stop and jot their ideas, and share those thoughts with the class. This question is complex and likely not one that has been given much thought to it before. It may unveil a belief system or mindset that has already been established by parents, teachers, and personal self-talk.

On the early elementary level, the question can simply focus on what is more important when trying to do better in school: recognizing strengths or working hard to fix weaknesses. It is very likely that most students, young and old, will struggle with the idea that you should place any and/or more emphasis on discovering and cultivating strengths.

Culturally, over time, schools have placed significant and profound emphasis that more time and attention should be devoted to *fixing* weaknesses rather than addressing strengths. It is a message students have been receiving directly and indirectly for quite some time. Failing an English class may possibly initiate a schedule change with the addition of an added English remedial class to address that weakness. Failing English results in two periods of your weakest subject, but getting an A in English will not likely find an additional period added to feed that passion.

The possibility that school should emphasize student strengths over weaknesses may have never occurred to students at all. The question will be left open-ended, as it will be revisited in this chapter and the next.

In order to better understand the question, students will be presented with eight character strengths that were identified by Chris Peterson and Martin Seligman in their book *Character Strengths and Virtues: A Handbook and Classification.* These strengths should be identified as qualities that all individuals possess to some degree. The following eight will be used in this abbreviated introduction: love of learning, kindness, bravery, fairness, forgiveness, hope, humor, and creativity (see teacher resources section).

Based on the age and ability of the students, these eight strengths may simply be presented, or they may require clarification and a discussion to determine understanding. These strengths should be posted in the room and given to each child in the form of cards to hold, look at, and, hopefully, begin to internalize their meanings.

With the reminder that individuals possess all of these qualities to some degree, students will be instructed to order them according to the perception of the personal strengths that they possess. In other words, the first word in their stack should be the quality most identified with, the second card should be the next quality they feel describes the individual's personal strengths, and so on. Consequently, the last strength (the eighth card) should be the weakest strength.

The first partnering activity will include sharing the order of your cards with a partner. Simply stating the order is not enough; students must explain why the card was placed high, in the middle, or low on their scale of strengths by providing specific examples from daily life. For example, a student might say they are forgiving because their little brother recently broke their favorite toy, and they didn't get angry because they knew it was an accident.

On the contrary, the student might put forgiving at the end of the list because after their little brother broke their favorite toy, despite realizing it was an accident, they held a grudge for days. Emphasis should be placed on purposeful placement of the cards with supporting evidence and personal stories. Once all students have had an opportunity to share, the class will come together to share the results.

In order to admire and appreciate the diversity of the class, a class word cloud will be designed using each student's top two strengths. The imagery should assist in noting which traits are more prevalent than others as well as providing information for more well-rounded partnerships in the future.

The book *Giraffes Can't Dance* will provide us with some insights on strength finding, via Gerald the giraffe. For Gerald, the question of which proves more important, discovering his strengths or focusing on his weaknesses, will provide a simplistic and obvious solution. The hope is that the book can inspire students to identify and harness personal strengths.

THE READ-ALOUD: STORIES THAT STICK

The students are now ready to engage in the read-aloud exploring the story in whatever format that the teacher chooses to share the story. Questions before, during, and after the reading are on the template and are provided merely as suggestions.

It is the belief of the authors that questions used to drive the reading are best created by the individual classroom teacher as part of the teachable moments that make read-aloud experiences come to life. More than likely, the suggestions will get you started and follow-up questions will arise in response to students' reactions.

SUMMATIVE PERFORMANCE TASK

In order to follow up on the reading, it is important to continue to reinforce the ability to recognize strengths in themselves as well as identify those qualities in others. Students will first take a VIA character strengths test online to formally identify their strengths and virtues.

This next activity improves the classroom climate, identifies individual strengths, and boosts self-esteem. The activity is called *Strength 360*, and it was developed out of the SMART Strengths Program and is provided here as a small indicator of a truly enriching and life-changing program. Each student in the class will be provided with a poster with a name on it, and the posters will be affixed around the perimeter of the room.

All of the students in the class participate by rotating around the room and writing down the strength (using the 24 identified in the VIA online survey) they believe their classmate possess. After all the students have filled in character traits on each poster, they will stand in front of their poster one by one. As they stand, each student will share the traits that they possess and what experiences helped them arrive at that conclusion.

It is vital that students share how they have come to choose that specific character trait. For example, a student might write kindness, but should explain, because "I saw Allison help a kindergartner who was lost find the bathroom." After the entire class has had an opportunity to write, each child will return to their own poster, and compare the findings on the VIA test with their classmates' beliefs. Often classmates will spot strengths not identified on the test.

Expect a degree of discomfort; people, young and old, are not used to being complimented in such a public way. Completing the lesson in this manner strives to send the message that it is OK to shine and that these strengths are recognized and appreciated by their classmates. After the completion of this activity, children should be comfortable with identifying the qualities associated with each strength and should begin to have a better gauge on their strengths as identified from peers.

Extension

The extension activity builds upon this by asking children to keep a weekly *strengths journal*. They will be encouraged to notice any patterns in the strengths people associate themselves with, keep track of compliments, note times when they feel *at their best*, and take notice of the qualities in them that seem to be uniquely theirs and set them apart from others.

Self-described "quirks" often provide insight into our strengths. The journaling activity can go on for as long as it seems beneficial. The goal is that students are able to note their strengths and feel confident they understand why that attribute is associated with their unique character. The *strengths journal* will also be used as a tool for completing the argument portion of this inquiry.

It is vitally important that the ideas of this lesson, that all children have strengths, be brought home and reinforced. An easy way to do this is to provide parents with the set of eight words and require the parents to identify two words from the list of strengths they believe their child has and why.

The results of this discussion can be recorded in the *strengths journal* as one of the first activities. It is critical that parents understand that all children have strengths and that the fostering and application of these strengths can inevitably be the path for their child's motivation and success at large.

Argument

In order to employ the rigor necessary in the era of Common Core, the following activity is suggested as a culminating activity to this inquiry. Student partnerships should be established deliberately. A partner should be a person the student knows fairly well. This could be because of friendships or maybe common experiences over a very long time.

Students must feel safe and comfortable to explore their strengths and being able to trust their partner is imperative. Once groupings are established, students will be presented with the assignment; the students will make a slideshow (Google slides or any other) that describes the two most dominant strengths of the assigned partner. Students will be required to identify the specific strength and provide proof in the form of various sources.

The supporting evidence must be persuasive and may be supplied via entries from the *strengths journal*, personal experiences, or interviews with classmates. In addition, the students will be required to identify a successful person who also embodies one of these qualities. Explanation must be provided that documents how the figure uses character strength to achieve their goals.

The level of auditory persuasion can depend on what skill set you would like to place more emphasis on. If presenting a persuasive argument, oral presentation is a priority; it might only be required that children have a graphic organizer to reference, as they make their case. If quality evidence is the focus, you may want all the supporting details listed clearly with substantial proof clearly identified. There is a tremendous amount of flexibility in order to allow the teacher to make appropriate modifications according to his or her needs.

TAKING INFORMED ACTION

The concept behind strengths needs to play a continued role in the classroom. Simply identifying your strengths is not enough to promote real change. Children can be encouraged to maintain strengths journals and participate in a monthly "pair and share" with classmates and/or their parents. When designing group activities in any subject area, strengths should be addressed as an obvious strategy for developing well-rounded grouping.

Students should be encouraged to offer their assistance to classmates. When doing so, students model how this particular strength can be utilized effectively. Coaching a classmate through an activity will not only reinforce the strength in the student assisting but will also aid the students requiring help through witnessing the self-talk of the model.

In schools that embrace professional Twitter accounts, students can be encouraged to report evidence of one of the eight character strengths in themselves or when they witness the strength in another. The hashtags could be the following:

- #characterstrengths
- #loveoflearning
- #humor
- #creativity

One of the wonderful side effects is simply a school-wide shift to recognizing the good in others.

At home, parents can be provided postcards. When witnessing their child thriving in a particular area, they can jot them a note with special attention to their identified strengths. This will encourage and reward the child through praise and recognition of their strengths. The combination of efforts should slowly create a shift in which children feel better and begin to recognize and employ their strengths.

Finally, if the class is an upper-level elementary classroom, they can become ambassadors of the character strengths and present the modified strengths activities done in their room to a younger grade. It is this hope that action will be the start of a movement that focuses school-wide attention and emphasis on student strengths.

Table 13.2. Sample VIA Strengths Chart

Love of Learning Mastering and enthusiasm for new skills, topics, and knowledge	**Kindness** Doing favors and good deeds for others
Bravery Not shrinking from a challenge; acting on convictions even if not popular	**Fairness** Treating all people the same; not letting personal feelings or bias decisions about others
Forgiveness Forgiving those who have done wrong; accepting the shortcomings of others	**Hope** Expecting the best in the future and working to achieve it
Humor Liking to laugh, bringing smiles to others, seeing the lighter side	**Creativity** Thinking of novel and productive ways to view things; imaginative

Chapter 14

Unleashing Strengths

Using Strengths to Discover the Best You

Dream Big, Little Pig! by Kristi Yamaguchi and Tim Bowers

HOW THIS BOOK CONNECTS TO POSITIVE PSYCHOLOGY RESEARCH ON CHARACTER STRENGTHS

Dream Big, Little Pig! provides a perfect connection to the grit research on *Iggy Peck, Architect*, presented in Section II C. The lesson contends that true passion for a goal is better achieved when an individual is pursuing a goal that arises from their unique strengths, talents, and affinities. After Poppy the pig moves through a series of failed attempts at areas of ballet and singing, she discovers her strength, figure skating. It is in this arena that Poppy discovers a unique "magic" that enables her to find her grit and arrive at flow.

Much of Duckworth's grit theory revolves around the need for deliberate practice, which is often depicted as rigorous, demanding, and focused work rather than joy and flow. This can be especially true when the activity develops out of a need for remedying a weakness. Deliberate practice is often focused practice on the facets of what individuals cannot do easily. When that practice is not based on a weakness, but on a strength, individuals have the potential to experience flow, optimal engagement.

Mihaly Csikszentmihalyi introduced the world to the idea of flow in his research in *Flow: The Psychology of Optimal Experience*. This research proposes that people are happiest when in a state of flow. Flow is a level of engagement that occurs when a person's talent or skill is at an optimal level for the task at hand. If the task is too easy, boredom results and flow will never be achieved. If the task is too difficult, anxiety and frustration will stifle flow. However, flow is far more than optimal engagement arising out of challenges. Flow is achieved when individuals pursue activities that they are passionate about that arise from strengths.

Flow is borne of love and has the power to make work to not seem like work, but rather feel more like rapture or joy. The state of flow consists of extreme concentration, engagement, and absorption. One experiencing flow is "in the zone," and nothing else seems to matter but the activity at hand.

Csikszentmihalyi describes a flow state almost as a state of suspended animation when focus becomes so purposeful that one can actually lose sight of time and space. Immersed in work so totally that the reward is the activity itself as actions and awareness merge into concentration so intense that we lose the sense of self. Flow is built when discovering and harnessing strengths, not when addressing dreaded weaknesses.

Students will identify the difference in Poppy when failing at ice-skating both in language and in pictures compared to when failing in other areas. Tom Rath, in a renowned TED talk, explains that parents and schools focus more on a child's grade of an F than the grade of an A. In all likelihood, the As will lead more directly to identifying a child's strengths than the Fs. The world is thankful that the book's author, Kristi Yamaguchi, found her As in ice-skating and followed those As.

More detailed information on character strengths research is available for teachers and parents in the reference section in Chapter 20 of this book. These shared sources on character strengths include YouTube presentations, life-altering books applying the research to daily life, and a snapshot of the scholarly research from which the positive psychology supporting the chapter has been derived. Teachers are encouraged to dig deeper into developing a rich understanding of the research in order to strengthen the power and delivery of the lesson.

Lesson Design: *Dream Big, Little Pig!*
Megan Pavlick

Table 14.1.   Using Strengths to Discover the Best You: *Dream Big, Little Pig!* by Kristi Yamaguchi and Tim Bowers

Compelling Question	Could finding our strength be the secret to getting *gritty*?
Common Core Standards	• CCSS.ELA-LITERACY.CCRA.R.2 • CCSS.ELA-LITERACY.CCRA.SL.1 • CCSS.ELA-LITERACY.CCRA.W.1 • NCSS—Theme 4: Individual Development and Identity • NCSS Inquiry Arc— Dimension 4

Staging the Question	Students will discuss the meaning of the Vincent van Gogh quote, "What is done in love is done well." The teacher will present famous images and background information on the famous artist relevant to the central theme of the book (sticking to your dreams and getting lost in creative flow).	

Supporting Question 1 (Before reading) What are more important your strengths or your weaknesses?	Supporting Question 2 (During reading) How does Poppy change when she discovers her strengths in Dream Big Little Pig!?	Supporting Question 3 (After reading) How do your character strengths and affinities affect your ability to persevere in the face of obstacles and live in flow?
Are you more successful when you use your strengths or when you fix your weaknesses? Are you more successful when you work hard or when you enjoy what you are doing? How does it feel when you are successful? How does it feel when you are doing a skill or activity that you are good at or that you enjoy? How does it feel when you are spending a lot of your time trying to fix your weaknesses? Describe a time when you got lost in doing something so enjoyable.	How do you think Poppy feels when she is told ballet, singing, and modeling "is just not for her"? What is a strength that you notice Poppy possesses? How do Poppy's mother, grandparents, and best friend Emma act as hope persuaders to Poppy? How do you know that Poppy is enjoying ice-skating? How do you think Poppy feels when she ice-skates? What does Poppy mean when she says ice-skating feels like magic? Why doesn't Poppy notice that she isn't perfect on the ice?	What does it mean to dream big? Did Poppy fail well? Was Poppy successful because she harnessed her strengths or fixed her weaknesses? When Poppy learned to ice-skate, she said it felt "like magic." How does Poppy ice-skate so well? What do you think magic feels like? Describe a skill or activity that feels like magic to you. Describe a skill or activity that is done well because it is done in love. Is the level of one's success related to the level of love and happiness involved when completing a skill or activity?
Formative Performance Task	Formative Performance Task	Formative Performance Task
Students will participate in answering questions that elicit where they are in regard to their views on the attainment and experience of success. Students will be presented with developmentally appropriate and relevant background information on Vincent van Gogh and the "what is done in love" quote. Students will share their "noticings" and thoughts on the meaning behind the quote.	Students will observe a think-aloud. Students will verbally share their inferences and "noticings" about Poppy throughout the reading of the text. Students will respond to the above questions at key points.	Students will paint or draw a metaphorical image of their "magic."

Continued

Table 14.1.   Continued

Featured Sources	Featured Sources	Featured Sources
Quote by Vincent van Gogh, "What is done in love is done well." Developmentally appropriate materials used to provide background information on Van Gogh, such as pictures of his famous paintings or a tribute video clip, "A Tribute to Vincent van Gogh" video, https://www.youtube.com/watch?v=XemwelAvi8Q.	*Dream Big Little Pig!* by Kristi Yamaguchi and Tim Bowers	Thick paper, watercolors, crayons, colored pencils (or other preferred artistic avenues)

Summative Performance Task	**Argument**	Students will write a brief rationale for their art piece explaining why they are successful when lost in their "magic." The written rationale may be a headline, a caption, or even a paragraph. Students will participate in a gallery walk of everyone's painted metaphors.
	Extension	Students will ask their parents to describe a skill or activity that they love doing and do well. Students will explain the metaphor of "magic" and ask their parents to illustrate their "magic."
Taking Informed Action (Enrichment)		Students will participate in a gallery walk of their parents' metaphors. Students will participate in a class discussion on the importance of harnessing strengths in adulthood for the success and happiness of one's self. Students will invite their personal paragons of flow and strengths to be part of the classroom gallery by submitting their stories.

STAGING THE LESSON

This lesson presents an opportunity for students to contemplate the compelling question, "could finding our strength be the secret to getting *gritty*?" In the opening discussion, the teacher should present students with questions to elicit where students are in regard to their views on the attainment and experience of success. The teacher should use questioning techniques suitable for the cognitive level of the students, while asserting a high level of expectations for student thinking. Younger students will require simplified and related questions that make this sophisticated question more accessible to their everyday experience.

The teacher might ask the following questions: *Are you more successful when you use your strengths or when you fix your weaknesses? Are you more successful when you work hard or when you enjoy what you are doing? How does it feel when you are successful? How does it feel when you are doing a skill or activity that you are good at or that you enjoy? How does it feel when you are spending a lot of your time trying to fix your weaknesses? Describe a time when you got lost in doing something so enjoyable.* It is the hope that the students are able to answer these questions openly and honestly.

These questions provide a powerful launch for the lesson as they set the stage for students to build a metacognitive connection to who they are as learners, thinkers, and successful people. If students tend to see effort or natural ability as the reasons for their success, it is important for the teacher to invite students down a new path of thought. *Is the level of one's success related to the level of love and happiness involved when completing a skill or activity?*

For many students, the direction of the questioning is clear, and for others, it may not be as obvious. Whatever the case may be, students should be given the chance to reflect on their own perception of success in relationship to happiness. The teacher should facilitate a deeper discussion about how it feels mentally and emotionally when exercising strengths or those things they love that come naturally.

The teacher can explain to the students that when a person makes use of a strength in a positive way, there is often enjoyment and success involved in the result. This, in turn, provides passion to the students that enable deliberate practice and *getting gritty* about their passions.

Providing real-life examples would be beneficial for the teacher to share with the students. For example, a teacher may share with students that when artists are drawing or painting, there is often no attention to time, appetite, or external distractions. When drawing or painting, the artist might make use of the character strengths of spirituality, creativity, and appreciation of beauty, and that this specific activity brings joy and fulfillment.

It would be beneficial for students to consider a connection between flow and success. Throughout this lesson, the teacher should embed this consideration in class discussions and student self-analysis. During the read-aloud, the students will later discover that Poppy experiences flow when she achieves her dream of becoming an ice-skater. This will offer the students the chance to make the connection between flow and success.

To illustrate the reality of flow and success in a person, the teacher can present the students with Vincent van Gogh and his famous quote, "what is done in love is done well." Although his success was realized after his death, Van Gogh found success through creative flow, hard work, demonstration of hope and grit, and self-awareness.

Younger students do not need to know the specific details of Van Gogh's deeply troubled life, as they are not necessary to make the connection between flow and success. However, a teacher may go into some detail of Van Gogh's constant rejection and internal suffering as this knowledge would add an additional layer of understanding of *The Starry Night* artist.

Biography.com sufficiently describes the rejection, isolation, and sorrow that Vincent experienced in his lifetime. His perseverance through failure was rooted in his passion for painting and nature, hard work ethic, and the hopeful support of his brother, Theo. Van Gogh used his character strengths of spirituality, appreciation of beauty, hope, love, persistence, and creativity to find success as a revolutionary painter in the post-impressionism period.

To reinforce his passionate and relentless approach in working toward his dreams, Van Gogh believed that "your profession is not what brings home your weekly paycheck, your profession is what you're put here on earth to do, with such passion and such intensity that it becomes spiritual in calling."

One tool a teacher may use when presenting background information on the artist to the students is an inspirational video. "A Tribute to Vincent van Gogh," found on youtube.com, is a visual montage of the artist's famous paintings set to the Don McLean song entitled "Vincent."

After providing the students with developmentally appropriate background information on the artist, the teacher should focus on his brief yet influential quote: "What is done in love is done well." The teacher can post the quote in front of the room or provide students with individual copies of the quote.

The teacher will facilitate a meaningful discussion where the students will be encouraged to share thoughts on the quote's meaning. The teacher will guide the students in recognizing that the more love and passion one has for a skill or activity, the greater success one will hopefully experience.

Once the students are introduced to the connection between success, strengths, and flow, they will now be prepared for the class read-aloud. The teacher will inform the students that they will read about a pig who dreams big and yearns for success.

THE READ-ALOUD: STORIES THAT STICK

The students are now ready to engage in the read-aloud exploring the story in whatever format that the teacher chooses to share the story. Questions before, during, and after the reading are on the template and are provided merely as suggestions.

It is the belief of the authors that questions used to drive the reading are best created by the individual classroom teacher as part of the teachable moments that make read-aloud experiences come to life. More than likely, the suggestions will get you started and follow-up questions will arise in response to students' reactions.

SUMMATIVE PERFORMANCE TASKS

When the read-aloud is complete, the teacher may introduce the following questions to promote deep thinking on the book's central theme: *What does it mean to dream big? Did Poppy fail well? Was Poppy successful because she harnessed her strengths or fixed her weaknesses?* The students will be encouraged to voice their thinking and support their thinking with both textual evidence and personal insight.

Students should understand that Poppy's failures were essential on the journey toward discovering her personal magic. It was because of the natural experience of failure that Poppy's strengths were realized. Whether or not Poppy knows that failure acts as a stepping stone to success, a reader can infer that Poppy knows how to fail well.

Students should be made aware that Poppy didn't spend extra time on fixing her weaknesses. Instead, she dedicated her time, passion, and energy toward finding the thing that brings her happiness. The ability to tolerate greater failure in doing ice-skating, which Poppy loved, should be made clear in the questioning.

At this time, the teacher should direct the discussion toward the pivotal moment when Poppy learned to ice-skate. The teacher may ask questions such as, *When Poppy learned to ice-skate, she said it felt "like magic." How does Poppy ice-skate so well? What do you think magic feels like?* During this discussion, the teacher should spend careful time on introducing and explaining Poppy's metaphorical representation of ice-skating as "magic."

The act of ice-skating was a magical experience for Poppy; therefore, magic is a metaphorical representation for her state of flow. Yamaguchi describes the enthusiastic skater as "so happy gliding and sliding and tumbling and bumbling on the ice, she didn't even notice that she wasn't perfect." This textual evidence leads the reader to believe that Poppy is in a complete state of absorption and happiness. Nothing else in the world matters more to Poppy than that exact moment of ice-skating with ease.

All of Poppy's hard work and perseverance paid off as she found her creative flow. Finding her strength fueled her grit. This flow and happiness brought Poppy much success on the ice. Not only was ice-skating a magical experience for her, it was her "magic." After students are done analyzing Poppy's strengths and road to success, it is important that they transition this analysis to their own lives.

This crucial transition will enhance their self-awareness in a needed period of self-discovery, and ultimately helps them to identify personal strengths and affinities. There are numerous ways in which a teacher may offer the students an opportunity to demonstrate an application of understanding.

One way in which the students can connect this story to their own self-discovery is to name a skill or activity that feels like magic. The teacher can remind the students of van Gogh's quote, "What is done in love is done well." The teacher can ask the students to describe a skill or activity that they do well because it is done in love. It is important that students are given ample time to truly reflect on the things that bring them happiness and in a state of flow.

After the students share aloud, the teacher will point out that these named skills or activities are the students' "magic." Depending upon the students' experience with figurative language, the teacher will provide the needed support for the students to understand the metaphorical relationship.

It is suggested that the teacher models his or her own painted metaphor (Diagram 1). For example, a teacher may share with students that when drawing, participation in this activity involves no attention to time, loss of appetite, or external distractions. When drawing, the teacher makes use of her character strengths of spirituality, creativity, and appreciation of beauty, and this specific activity brings joy and fulfillment.

This act of drawing might be defined as the "magic" in life. Whether the teacher paints the metaphor in front of the students or prior to the lesson, it is beneficial for students to see the teacher experience the task they are about to participate in so that they know what it looks like and sounds like to complete the task.

Argument

The students are ready for the formative performance task of painting a personal metaphorical magic picture in a reflection journal. The students will paint themselves doing the skill or activity that brings absorption, engagement, and happiness. The teacher will inform the students that their named skill or activity is something that will hopefully bring success in life if it has not already.

The Project Zero Classroom at the Harvard Graduate School of Education nurtures a culture of thinking through the use of visible thinking routines. Lisa Verkerk emphasizes the importance of developing students' dispositions to be reflective. One way Verkerk suggests that a teacher can promote reflectiveness in the learning environment is through the use of reflection journals.

Painted reflection journals provide opportunities for ongoing assessments for the teacher and self-assessment for the students. These student-painted metaphors will serve as personal reflections in response to the theories behind the lesson's story. Once the metaphors are painted, students should write a brief rationale for the art piece explaining the success that results when lost in flow (personal magic zone).

Figure 14.1. Example of Flow Drawing by Megan Pavlick

The written rationale may be a headline, a caption, or even a paragraph. The teacher should make that decision based on student ability, need, and time. For hesitant writers, the experience of painting the metaphor first should provide a drafted confidence when formulating ideas into words.

Hesitant writers can verbalize a personal rationale when viewing the painted metaphor and then put the verbalization into writing. Prior to the students' writing, it is important that the teacher also model a personal rationale for the students so that they see and hear how the task should look and sound.

For example, the teacher can post her painted metaphor for the students to view, and model the thinking behind the painting aloud and generate a written rationale to represent the meaning behind the metaphor. The teacher may say, "My magic is when I am immersed in my artistic expression. My crayons, markers, and pencils are my creative tools to express my admiration for the love in my life. I experience flow when I am drawing and this brings me happiness and success."

The students will now generate individual rationales to explain the created metaphors. Students will participate in a gallery walk viewing and taking notes on the painted metaphors. The gallery walk should be a reverent and appreciative viewing into the lives and perspectives among peers.

Extension

The lesson can have a long-lasting effect upon the learner when it extends beyond the lesson. Students can bring this application home to get parents involved in the story's analysis of success. The students will ask parents to describe a skill or activity that their parents love doing and do well.

Students will explain the metaphor of "magic" from *Dream Big Little Pig!* and ask their parents to illustrate the personal "magic" that has been revealed in the lesson. Students and parents can discuss and answer the question, *Is the level of one's success related to the level of love and happiness involved when completing a skill or activity?* With their parents engaged in the same task that the children performed in school, it is likely that the students grow even more invested in the lesson's book and compelling question.

TAKING INFORMED ACTION

In order to make this inquiry long-lasting in the students' lives, it is important that they take an action that connects their classroom inquiry to the outside world. One way to connect their classroom with the outside world is by asking their parents to create their magic metaphor. When the students return their parents' metaphors to school, they can have a gallery walk of their parents' metaphors.

Students will be able to circulate the room and see that the adults in their lives also have strengths and passions that are used to bring success and happiness. The teacher will facilitate a class discussion on the importance of harnessing strengths and applying grit in adulthood for the success and happiness.

Students may post both student and parent metaphors on a bulletin board in the school hallway so that other students and teachers can celebrate the strengths and passions of peers within a school community. If others show appreciation for one's strengths and passions, it is more likely that they may serve as hope persuaders when life gets challenging.

It is the intention of this lesson for students to grapple with the source of success and to immerse themselves into self-analysis in relationship to success. After building a gallery of strengths and passions in the room, students can identify the most athletes, celebrities, or leaders who offer they are inspired by. Students can write to their personal inspirational flow paragons, sharing the story of Poppy and the classroom gallery, asking the celebrity to join the wall by filling out a sheet inquiring about their personal magic, or even drawing their own picture.

This lesson also serves as a permanent invitation for students to constantly consider the call to use their strengths. Hopefully, students will walk away with the confidence to be guided by their personal and unique strengths and passions, taking another step closer to success.

Chapter 15

Synergy

The Power of Combining Your Strengths with Others

> *Going Places* by Paul A. Reynolds and Peter H. Reynolds

HOW THIS BOOK CONNECTS TO POSITIVE PSYCHOLOGY RESEARCH ON CHARACTER STRENGTHS

Building on the two previous stories infusing character strengths through children's literature, *Going Places* hammers home the power of synergy and the necessity of combining our strengths with others. The ability to combine strengths to form a more synchronous world is vital if we wish to effectively address the overwhelming problems that face our world.

Through the compelling question, *Going Places* infuses the critical message that we are all not necessarily well rounded, but we are all unique and possess defining and powerful character strengths. Though students may strive to be well rounded, it is our special talents and ways of looking at the world that may best help children find success in life. *Going Places* teaches children to celebrate strengths, rather than only dwell and focus only on weaknesses.

Tom Rath in his address to the 2015 World Conference on Positive Psychology asserted that "the best leaders in the world are not well-rounded, but great teams are." This insight seems to be lost on most of America's schools as it seeks to instill the belief in every student that they must be expert in all endeavors and disciplines. This mandate that every child be well rounded runs counter to human experience, which teaches us that the surest path to success is built on our defined strengths and affinities.

In Tom Rath's latest book, *Are You Fully Charged*, a strengths-based prescription for successful life is offered. Rath suggests that to flourish individuals need *positive relationships*, interactions with others, *health*, the secrets of eating, sleeping, and moving right, and, finally, *meaning* to thrive. The *meaning* part is best found by harnessing one's individual strengths, interests, with the needs of others in the world.

Students must find what the world is calling them to do. This model for a life that enables one to flourish is in the best traditions of Martin Seligman, the founder of field of positive psychology. Seligman defines a life characterized by well-being as consisting of purpose, flow, and, to some degree, pleasure. Raphael and Maya offer a blueprint for well-being in combining their strengths to create a new idea and, in doing so, improve the world.

Much of positive psychology dealt to this point has been the application of the research principles to education. Readers should know that this is but a small snapshot of the application of this research. Positive psychology research is transforming businesses radically and with the same force as education. The parallel between business and schools is that both often work on a deficit model, which focuses on what an individual, organization, or a school lacks.

David Cooperrider, of Case Western University, in his groundbreaking work, *Appreciative Inquiry*, makes the point that business models also focus on what's wrong rather than what's right. In *Appreciative Inquiry*, Cooperrider makes the case for a new business design model built on defining and employing the unique strengths of an organization rather than its weaknesses.

The Positive Organization and *Deep Change*, by Robert Quinn, are two of many texts that highlight the radical transformation of businesses that is taking place through appreciative inquiry. This model has been applied dramatically around the world, not only in business organizations, but even in United Nations' efforts to build synergy between world religions.

In Cooperrider's *Appreciative Inquiry* model, change is focused on four strengths-based directions referred to as *discovery, dream, design*, and *destiny*. Operating from a strengths perspective, organizations must first *discover* what is done well and what is at the heart of the best that we are as an organization, the defined strengths of the organization.

The *dream* focus is on imagining what the world is calling us to do. *Design* involves co-constructing our ideal organization based on our defined strengths to help us provide what the world needs. *Destiny* relates to how we learn, empower, and adjust to bring our new vision to life.

This design "go-cart" model in *Going Places* brought to life a new design, which originated from strengths and imagination. It was created by what the world might be calling two very different individuals to do. It's a perfect place to introduce the idea of strengths beyond the classroom into the curriculum.

More detailed information on character strengths research is available for teachers and parents in the reference section in Chapter 20 of this book. These shared sources on character strengths include YouTube presentations, life-altering books applying the research to daily life, and a snapshot of the scholarly research from which the positive psychology supporting the chapter has been derived. Teachers are encouraged to dig deeper into developing a rich understanding of the research in order to strengthen the power and delivery of the lesson.

Lesson Design: *Going Places*
Angela Abend

Table 15.1. The Power of Combining Your Strengths with Others: *Going Places* by Paul A. Reynolds and Peter H. Reynolds

Compelling Question	Does everyone have to be well rounded?
Common Core Standards	• CCSS.ELA-LITERACY.CCRA.R.2 • CCSS.ELA-LITERACY.CCRA.SL.1 • CCSS.ELA-LITERACY.CCRA.W.l • NCSS—Theme 4: Individual Development and Identity • NCSS Inquiry Arc— Dimension 4
Staging the Question	After discussing the directions, students will try the Nine-Dot Challenge. Once solution is established, students will view the Nine-Dot Challenge video and discuss the challenge and individuals who are out of the box.

Supporting Question 1 (Before reading) What does it mean to be an out-of-the-box thinker?	*Supporting Question 2 (During reading) What are the differences in strengths between Rafael and Maya in Going Places? What happens when they combine those strengths?*	*Supporting Question 3 (After reading) What is the result of combining our strengths with the strengths of others (synergy)?*
Can do you draw four lines to connect nine dots without retracing or picking up your pencil from the paper? • • • • • • • • •	How do Maya and Rafael think differently when completing a challenge? What do you predict Rafael will do when he notices how Maya designs her go-cart for the Going Places competition? What should he do? What would you do? Why? Have you ever had to work with a partner with that thought and acted in completely different ways? How did you handle it? Did it work out? Why or why not?	Do you connect more with Rafael or Maya when completing a challenge? Why? Is a combination of BOTH ways of thinking ideal? Why did a better product emerge? How do group projects change when you have people who think differently? In which type of group do you think does the better work in the end? Should someone have to give up their strengths to get along in a group?

Continued

Table 15.1. Continued

Formative Performance Task	Formative Performance Task	Formative Performance Task
Students will complete the challenge above. They will participate in a discussion on how one must follow the directions and "think outside the box" in order to successfully solve the challenge. This leads to a discussion that some people may be considered "out of the box," but they could have the best solutions in life. Often these people follow strengths that are outside the box.	Students respond to the above questions at key points in the text.	After reading and discussing *Going Places*, the students will complete the "Marshmallow Challenge" (©Tom Wujeck) in groups of four.

Featured Sources	Featured Sources	Featured Sources
Nine-Dot Challenge Explanation: https://www.youtube.com/watch?v=SgWF-nV5kZk	*Going Places* by Peter and Paul Reynolds Book Trailer at: https://www.youtube.com/watch?v=0uxq6d7Q180	http://www.tomwujec.com/designprojects/marshmallow-challenge/ http://marshmallowchallenge.com/Welcome.html https://goo.gl/7CvILl

Summative Performance Task		
	Argument	Students will write a response to the questions: *Is it important to have contributions from both Rafael's and Maya's ways of thinking when completing a group challenge? Why or why not? Give text evidence and outside examples to support your thinking.*
	Extension	The students will take one or two lines from his or her response and place them on the *Going Places* bulletin board in classroom and then tweet them on the class Twitter account under the hashtag #teamgoingplaces.

Taking Informed Action (Enrichment)	Students will form classroom groupings that involve groups made up of individuals possessing radically diverse character strengths and personalities.
	Students will learn about the *Appreciative Inquiry* model, pioneered by David Cooperrider of Case Western University. This model seeks to inspire change in business by focusing on what businesses do well rather than weaknesses. Students will write to and connect with these innovators.
	Based on the desire of the teacher and the students, the class will employ the discover, dream, design, and sustain *Appreciative Inquiry* models to solve a schoolwide or class problem. These models will be *presented at open board meetings to the Board of Education.*

STAGING THE LESSON

The celebration of creative thinking and collaborative spirit between Maya and Rafael captures what educators hope to foster in a classroom that truly embraces challenges. The students in this lesson truly learn to "share strengths" in order to "go places." After listening to the directions, each student will be presented with the Nine-Dot Challenge. Students will be encouraged to continue to try a plethora of times to complete it according to the guidelines.

When confronted with the Nine-Dot Challenge, students often say, "You didn't say we could draw the lines outside the box." This comment is key to a class discussion of looking at solutions from different perspectives and, literally, "thinking outside of the box." Students sometime feel tricked by the problem, but the discussion that follows should center on the necessity and often overlooked importance of those who think differently. This should build on the understanding that all individuals possess unique character strengths and capacities fostered in the last two books.

The Nine-Dot Challenge is an excellent lead-in to the concept of Maya's ways of thinking, while Rafael is also given a nod with respect to the guidelines that must be followed for its successful completion. Initial questions on Maya and Rafael might focus on the different strengths and ways of seeing the world that both possess.

After the questioning draws out the differences, the focus should be geared toward the ability to "share their strengths" to make ideas merge. In doing so, both Maya and Raphael eventually soar, together, at the great "Going Places" contest. Questioning should seek to relate this discussion to the personal experiences of the learners. Although they "soar" in the end, the reader can use personal experience to develop theories about how both probably had to struggle to find mutual respect.

THE READ-ALOUD: STORIES THAT STICK

The students are now ready to engage in the read-aloud exploring the story in whatever format that the teacher chooses to share the story. Questions before, during, and after the reading are on the template and are provided merely as suggestions.

It is the belief of the authors that questions used to drive the reading are best created by the individual classroom teacher as part of the teachable moments that make read-aloud experiences come to life. More than likely, the suggestions will get you started and follow-up questions will arise in response to students' reactions.

SUMMATIVE PERFORMANCE TASKS

After the read-aloud, students will be given the necessary materials needed for the Marshmallow Challenge and be placed into groups of three or four. This challenge is logistically simple: in 18 minutes, teams must build the tallest freestanding structure out of 20 sticks of spaghetti, one yard of tape, one yard of string, and one standard-sized marshmallow.

The unharmed marshmallow must rest steadily on top of the freestanding structure without the assistance of team members. In order to meet with success, students must work collaboratively, think critically and creatively, and communicate effectively. For more specific information and helpful hints in administering the Marshmallow Challenge, see http://www.tomwujec.com/design-projects/marshmallow-challenge/.

Open-ended scenarios and challenges, such as the Marshmallow Challenge, allow students the opportunity to collaborate and "share strengths while honoring differences." A classroom must be the birthplace of synergy, but it must simultaneously be an honored workspace for both innovation and invention. A classroom culture that allows for the freedom to "think, make, and do" TOGETHER will provide the Rafaels and Mayas the skills and the strength needed to certainly "go places" that we, today, can't even begin to imagine.

Argument

Students will write a response to the questions: *Is it important to have both Rafael's and Maya's ways of thinking when completing a group challenge? Why or why not? Give text evidence and outside examples to support your thinking.* The students will be encouraged to consider whether groups function better when made up of Maya's and Rafael's way of thinking or when they are more congruent in strengths.

Extension

On a class Twitter account, students may tweet out responses to the summative question, *Is it important to have both Rafael's and Maya's ways of thinking when completing a group challenge? Why or why not?* under the #teamgoingplaces hashtag or an appropriate hashtag determined by the class. An alternative to the use of social media would be to post student responses on a *Going Places* bulletin board within the classroom.

TAKING INFORMED ACTION

Students will form classroom groupings that involve groups made up of students with diverse character strengths. After learning about David Cooperrider's *Appreciative Inquiry* model, student groups will write to one of the companies in the book that underwent change using the model. With this deep understanding of the *Appreciative Inquiry* process in place, students will be motivated to employ the model to make their own strengths-based change in the school or in the classroom.

Employing the *Appreciative Inquiry* model, pioneered by David Cooperrider, students will discover, dream, design, and sustain a new model of a school focused on strengths and the synergy of strengths rather than weaknesses. These models may be presented at school board meetings to the Board of Education.

As educators moving forward in the twenty-first century, we must ensure that students know *how* to think critically and constructively *while collaborating* to effectively and creatively communicate this constant stream of information. Some students will process this ever-flowing input with the keen eyes of a Rafael, while others will embrace it with a tremendous heart of Maya. Either way, or even more so, in both ways, a strength is developed that will truly allow all of our students to go "above and beyond."

Even more important is providing the setting for the development for new, innovative ideas beyond the confines of traditional curricula. "Flying go-carts" will be built only in environments that allow students to not only fail, but to "fail well." Classrooms that are courageous enough to offer challenges that let out-of-the-box strengths emerge find a place for both the Mayas and Rafaels of the world.

Section II E: Finding Happiness: Unlocking the Secrets of Happiness

Chapter 16

Discovering the Secret of Happiness
Doing for Others

How Full Is Your Bucket? For Kids by Tom Rath and Mary Reckmeyer

---

HOW THIS BOOK CONNECTS TO POSITIVE PSYCHOLOGY RESEARCH ON HAPPINESS

How Full Is Your Bucket? is a book that reveals to children the happiness generated by eudemonia: what we do for others. Sonja Lyubomirsky, one of the world's preeminent scholars on happiness, reveals that most people are on a hedonic treadmill, seeking the next personal pleasure or accomplishment. This striving for personal goals can make life feel like an unfulfilling race on a never-ending treadmill to reach the next hedonic plateau.

The belief that winning the lottery will result in ultimate happiness and losing a limb will make one miserable has been debunked in a number of positive psychology research studies. Research reveals that lottery winners will get a bump in happiness, but the bump is short-lived. In the same way that amputees will drop in happiness after losing a leg, with time, individuals will adjust to the loss of a limb as the new norm and happiness will return to the old levels. The bumps in happiness generally last an average of two years.

Lyubomirsky's key finding is that humans hedonically adapt to most of the attained goals. Eventually the new level of wealth brought about by the lottery win does not provide lasting happiness. Instead, individuals adapt and seek newer, greater goals to replace the old adapted to ones. Even acquiring the love of one's life can be adapted to after a two-year period. Individuals attain a desired goal and then begin almost immediately to desire even more.

What is it that makes us happy? Research indicates that eudemonic happiness, doing for others, provides more lasting happiness and fulfilling happiness than hedonic happiness. Based on Lyubomirsky's research, 50 percent of our happiness is determined by genetics and only a mere 10 percent by life circumstances or what happens to us. The other 40 percent is derived from how we react to the events of life and create meaning in life.

The How of Happiness shares Lyubomirsky's secrets on happiness and 12 tips for increasing your happiness on a daily basis. However, much of her research centers on gratitude. Being grateful and savoring what we have rather than being miserable about what is lacking is a key to finding happiness.

The book *How Full Is Your Bucket?* is a perfect story for sharing the power that individuals have to fill the bucket of those around them through positive comments and actions. The events in the book not only share how damaging negative comments are but also empower the reader by sharing the insight that individuals can control their interactions with others. In effect, based on the research on happiness, this control arms with the power to be happy by doing for others.

If doing for others creates eudemonic happiness, *How Full Is Your Bucket?* provides a strategy for all students to build happier lives. The filling of fellow classmates' buckets not only provides an anti-bullying message, but it also offers an antidote that can make students personally happier in the process. The powerful lesson of the book is that students can live a happier life by doing for others and filling the buckets of who make up their world.

More detailed information on happiness research is available for teachers and parents in the reference section in Chapter 20 of this book. These shared sources on happiness include YouTube presentations, books that can change your life, and scholarly research from which the positive psychology supporting the chapter has been derived.

Lesson Design: *How Full Is Your Bucket? For Kids*
Faith Tripp

Table 16.1. Doing for Others: *How Full Is Your Bucket? For Kids* by Tom Rath and Mary Reckmeyer

Compelling Question	What is it that makes us happy?
Common Core Standards	• CCSS.ELA-LITERACY.CCRA.R.2 • CCSS.ELA-LITERACY.CCRA.SL.1 • CCSS.ELA-LITERACY.CCRA.W.1 • NCSS—Theme 4: Individual Development and Identity • NCSS Inquiry Arc—Dimension 4
Staging the Question	**5–7 days prior:** In order to prepare for the lesson, students will receive a class list with space beside each student's name. Students will be provided with 30–45 minutes of quiet time where they will write one positive character trait for each student on the list. **Optional:** The class will co-construct an anchor chart with a list of positive character traits that can be used as a reference. Using the lists, individual word clouds will be created. **Hook/Lead:** Each student and allowing them to read, reflect, and discuss their reaction to their individual word cloud with a partner or small group.

Supporting Question 1 (Before reading) How can we show people that we care and support them?	*Supporting Question 2 (During reading) How do we empty someone's bucket or fill someone's bucket?*	*Supporting Question 3 (After reading) How does filling someone else's bucket make us feel happy?*
"We can do no great things; only small things with great love."—Blessed Teresa of Calcutta What does this quote mean to you? How did you feel after receiving the word cloud? Would you consider the word cloud a small thing or a great thing? Why? How can we show someone that we care about him or her? Is the secret to happiness found in giving or receiving?	Have you ever noticed your invisible bucket? How did Felix feel after he spilled his cereal and the dog ate his muffin? How does he feel on the bus and at school after the students are not kind to him? How do you feel when your bucket is almost empty? How do you begin to think and behave with an empty bucket? After Felix reads his story to the class, how do his feelings change? As Felix becomes more aware of other people's buckets, how does it change his thoughts and behaviors? How does it affect his bucket?	Is the secret to happiness found in giving or receiving? Why do we feel so good when we do something positive for someone else? How can we be bucket fillers?

Continued

Table 16.1. Continued

Formative Performance Task	Formative Performance Task	Formative Performance Task
Students will discuss the quote. After receiving their word clouds, students will brainstorm a list of small ways that they can show someone that they care about him or her.	Throughout the story, students will "Turn and Talk" with a partner to discuss the answers to the supporting questions and to share their text-to-self connections. Students will complete the "Drips from My Bucket" and "Drops in My Bucket" graphic organizers.	Students will view the Street Compliments video by the SoulPancake Street Team. Students will create a bucket-filling station in the classroom.

Featured Sources	Featured Sources	Featured Sources
Quote by Blessed Teresa of Calcutta Individual word clouds Free word cloud generator websites: www.wordle.net www.tagxedo.com www.wordclouds.com tagul.com	*How Full Is Your Bucket? for Kids* by Tom Rath and Mary Reckmeyer "Drips from My Bucket" and "Drops in My Bucket" double-sided graphic organizers	"Bucket-Filling Deeds" handout Bucket-filling station in classroom Street Compliments video by SoulPancake Street Team https://www.youtube.com/watch?v=-OBgdoAmuwI

Summative Performance Task	Argument	Students will write a gratitude letter to someone special in their life.
	Extension	Make a public service announcement (PSA) video that depicts bucket filling and bucket dipping at school and at home. Students will work in small groups to write scripts and produce the PSA. The videos can be uploaded to the school's website with parental permission.
Taking Informed Action (Enrichment)		**Understand:** Create a bucket-filling station in the classroom. Students can continuously add ideas for deeds that are bucket fillers. **Act:** Students will select an idea from the bucket-filling station and try to complete the task within the next few days. Each time they remove an idea, they must replace it with another one. **Assess:** Students will maintain an interactive notebook that contains reflections on their bucket-filling deeds.

STAGING THE LESSON

In an attempt to whet the students' appetites and encourage thoughtful reflection on the compelling question, students will be actively involved in an activity that includes positive giving and receiving. They will receive individualized word clouds that highlight their personal positive character traits according to their classmates.

A few days before the lesson, the teacher should provide each student with a class list with space beside each student's name. The students' task is to write one positive trait for each of their classmates on the list. The teacher should not reveal the end product of this activity but, instead, allow the word cloud to be a surprise hook in the coming days. If the students are young or are struggling with ideas, the class can work together to create an anchor chart that lists positive character traits.

The students can refer to the anchor chart as they complete the activity. This activity can take anywhere from 30 to 45 minutes. Once the lists are complete, the teacher should use the information to create individual word clouds for each student. Because creating the word clouds can be time consuming, the teacher should allow at least a week between this activity and the launch of the read-aloud.

Word clouds are fairly quick and simple to make, and there are a variety of websites that allow the user to generate free word clouds such as wordle.net, wordclouds.com, tagxedo.com, and tagul.com. Once the word clouds have been generated and are ready for distribution, the lesson can begin.

In order to hook the students, the teacher should post the following quote by Blessed Teresa of Calcutta: "We can do no great things; only small things with great love." The teacher will then distribute the word clouds and allow the students time to read, reflect, and discuss their reactions with a classmate or small group.

Next, the students should turn their attention to the quote and discuss the first supporting question: *What does this quote mean to you?* Student responses should be recorded on a large chart paper or on an interactive whiteboard. Then, the class will discuss the follow-up questions. *How did you feel after receiving the word cloud? Would you consider the word cloud a small thing or a great thing? Why?*

If the students have not yet made the connection, they will be reminded that the word clouds were made using their contributions from the previous week. After that, the class will quickly brainstorm and jot a list of ideas in response to the following question: *How can we show someone that we care about him or her?* Finally, the students will discuss the question, *What is it that makes us happy?*

THE READ-ALOUD: STORIES THAT STICK

The students are now ready to engage in the read-aloud exploring the story in whatever format that the teacher chooses to share the story. Questions before, during, and after the reading are on the template and are provided merely as suggestions.

It is the belief of the authors that questions used to drive the reading are best created by the individual classroom teacher as part of the teachable moments that make read-aloud experiences come to life. More than likely, the suggestions will get you started and follow-up questions will arise in response to students' reactions.

SUMMATIVE PERFORMANCE TASK

Argument

After the reading, students will view the video "An Experiment in Gratitude: The Science of Happiness" on YouTube (https://www.youtube.com/watch?v=oHv6vTKD6lg).

In keeping with the compelling question, "Is the secret to happiness found in giving or receiving?" the students will write and share a gratitude letter with a person who has been very influential in their life.

The purpose of this letter is to think deeply about someone who has done something really amazing or is important for the student and respond to that kindness with a letter of thanks. Allow the students ample time to reflect on the person and encourage them to write as much as they can about the person on the graphic organizer. Students should be reminded to include specific details and describe how those actions made them feel.

Depending on the grade level, students should review the standard structure of a friendly letter. After that, the students will take the information from their graphic organizers and use it to write a detailed gratitude letter. Because these letters are personal in nature, the student can elect whether or not to allow the teacher to read the content. The student can also elect whether or not to share the letter with the intended recipient, but they should be encouraged to share it if possible.

The act of sharing the letter is essential to fully understanding the compelling question as the answer is twofold: happiness is found in both giving *and* receiving. After the students have written and/or delivered the gratitude letters, they should reflect upon how it made them feel. This can take place in a small group or whole-class discussion. It is vital for the students to reflect on their feelings after the activity because it continues to build upon the understanding of the compelling question.

For younger students, it is suitable to complete an illustration of the special person. Younger students may also dictate their letter to the teacher, who will act as a scribe.

Extension

It is important for the students to take what they have discovered about the secret to happiness and share that "secret" with as many people as possible. A great way for students to share what they have learned and invite others to reflect on the question *What is it that makes us happy?* is to make short PSA videos.

These videos should depict instances of both bucket filling and bucket dipping at school and at home. The teacher should ensure that an equal number of videos depict bucket filling and bucket dipping. Students can work in small groups to write scripts and produce the PSA. Each student should play an important role in the creation and production of the video.

If a student is shy, he or she can work behind the camera and serve as the videographer, location scout, or prop designer. The videos should include the imagery of bucket drips and drops. In addition, the recipient's thoughts and feelings should be clearly expressed in order to drive home the idea of bucket dipping and bucket filling and the impact of each. The videos can be uploaded to the school's website with parental permission. They can also be shared at a school-wide assembly.

TAKING INFORMED ACTION

In order to allow students to demonstrate understanding, the teacher will create an interactive bucket-filling station in the classroom. The students will generate original ideas of positive deeds that can serve as bucket fillers and will place them in the class bucket or attach them to the bucket-filling station bulletin board.

Then, students will select random deeds from the station and attempt to carry them out within a few days. Once they select a deed, they must replace it with another original idea or resubmit the idea they selected if it was successful. This will be a continual practice throughout the unit.

After completing the deed, students will reflect upon the experience and share personal feelings in an interactive notebook. They may choose to address the reflection to parents, teachers, or a classmate. It is important to ensure that the intended recipient is aware of the letter and responds to it in a timely manner. The teacher will use the students' reflections in their interactive notebooks to continue to monitor and assess the students' understanding.

Gratitude Letter Graphic Organizer

The purpose of this letter is to think deeply about someone who has done something really amazing or important in your life. Respond to that kindness with a letter of thanks. Be sure to include specific details and your feelings.

Bucket-Filling Deed Slips

The students should use these slips to record original ideas of positive deeds that can serve as bucket fillers. They should place the slips in the class bucket or attach them to the bucket-filling station bulletin board. *Younger students can illustrate their ideas.

Whom am I writing to?	
What did he or she do?	How did it make me feel?

Figure 16.1.   Gratitude Letter Graphic Organizer

Bucket-Filling Deed	Bucket-Filling Deed
_____ _____ _____ _____	_____ _____ _____ _____
Bucket-Filling Deed	* Bucket-Filling Deed

Figure 16.2. Bucket-Filling Slips

How has someone dipped from your bucket?	How did that make you feel?	What did you do about it?
Illustration		

Figure 16.3. Drops from My Bucket

When have you dipped from someone else's bucket?	How did it make you feel?	What could you have done differently?
Illustration		

Figure 16.3.   Continued

How has someone filled your bucket?	How did that make you feel?	What did you do about it?
Illustration		

Figure 16.4.   Drips in My Bucket

How have you added a drop to someone else's bucket?	How did it make you feel?	How did it make the other person feel? How do you know?
Illustration		

Figure 16.4. Continued

Chapter 17

Finding Happiness in Your Life

The Power of Savoring

The Wise Woman and Her Secret by Eve Merriam and Linda Graves

HOW THIS BOOK CONNECTS TO POSITIVE PSYCHOLOGY RESEARCH ON HAPPINESS

The Wise Woman and Her Secret is a book that reveals to children the nature of savoring. Savoring is the process of truly being in the moment, being mindful, and experiencing gratitude for the heightened sense of pleasure that the joys of existence provide. This children's book shares with its readers deep insights on the essence of happiness in a story that allegorically portrays the inability of many to see the beauty in life that surrounds us.

In the story, the townspeople seek from the wise woman the secret of her wisdom and the secrets of a happy life. The townspeople are impatient with the woman when they ask her for her secret, and she tells them that "she cannot tell them, but they can look." This simple statement provides a deep insight that metaphorically reveals the townspeople's lack of awareness for the beauty and magic of life that surrounds them.

The townspeople's rush to seek out the mystery and beauty of life in pursuit of happiness ignores the obvious that many of us miss. The mystery of life surrounds all of us, but we are often too focused on the future to see it. Too often, individuals believe happiness will come only after attaining certain goals. Individuals postpone happiness believing it will arrive with a future event or circumstances. *The Wise Woman and Her Secret* teaches children that the seeds of happiness are all around us every day, if only we have the wisdom to appreciate and *savor* them.

163

Sonja Lyubomirsky explores this research deeply in *The Myths of Happiness*. Her research reveals that most of what people believe will make them happy does not and often what they feel will make them unhappy makes them happy. Marriage, having or finding the right partner, getting the right job, and even getting rich are goals that are commonly associated with happiness.

Research reveals, however, that these goals generally result in a two-year bump in happiness and individuals come to view the events as the new norm and return to levels of happiness prior to the goal attainment. The townspeople are in such a frenzy to discover the secret of life that they are unable to process the wisdom of the wise woman's words. The secrets of happiness are in savoring all that surrounds them.

When the wise woman tells the townspeople that they must discover the secret for themselves, her wisdom is that people are the sources of their own happiness. Savoring, an extreme form of mindfulness and gratitude, opens people to the beauty and excellence that are our world. Lyubomirsky's book *The How of Happiness* shares suggestions for living in the moment and experiencing gratitude.

Although the townspeople are oblivious to the message of the wise woman and the story, the young girl, Jenny, is not. In an almost dreamlike way, Jenny is immune to the frenzy and frustration that possess the townspeople. Instead, Jenny is captivated by the sensory wonder of everyday experience.

When Jenny lingers with the wise woman, after the townspeople have left, feeling a sense of frustration and failure, the secret is revealed. The secret is that the wisdom of life is contained in savoring the moment and appreciating the gift of life with all of its wonder and beauty.

The story is allegorical in that mankind's quest for happiness is shaped by the misguided assumption that happiness will come only after a future goal is attained. Students should fully engage the senses as Jenny does and be mindful of the beauty of the moment that defines existence.

More detailed information on happiness research is available for teachers and parents in the reference section in Chapter 20 of this book. These shared sources on happiness include YouTube presentations, books that can change your life, and scholarly research from which the positive psychology supporting the chapter has been derived.

Lesson Design: *The Wise Woman and Her Secret*
Edward Kemnitzer

Table 17.1. The Power of Savoring: *The Wise Woman and Her Secret* **by Eve Merriam and Linda Graves**

Compelling Question	What does it mean to savor?
Common Core Standards	• CCSS.ELA-LITERACY.CCRA.R.2 • CCSS.ELA-LITERACY.CCRA.SL.1 • CCSS.ELA-LITERACY.CCRA.W.1 • NCSS—Theme 4: Individual Development and Identity • NCSS Inquiry Arc—Dimension 4
Staging the Question	The students will view a video clip from *The Secret Life of Walter Mitty* and discuss reasons why the photographer doesn't take the picture when he had the perfect shot. They will debate why he made this decision.

Supporting Question 1 (Before reading) What does it mean to savor?	Supporting Question 2 (During reading) Why does the old woman in the book feel that the little girl in the story has found the secret of happiness in the Wise Woman?	Supporting Question 3 (After reading) What is the secret of happiness that the Wise Woman reveals to us?
What moments in life make people happy? Do the moments have to be major events or could they be minor details of daily life? Do we ever truly think about this concept of happiness on a daily basis? Do we lose sight of our happiness when we get older and lose our innocence? Do we value the beauty of nature around us? During which moments do we think about and value the nature around us? What does savoring mean to you? When have you savored experiences?	According to the author, what could provide "fortune" to the townspeople? Why does Jenny fall behind in the journey to find the secret of wisdom? What impact does her age have on her actions? Using evidence from the book, describe the wise woman's disposition. How does it differ from the other characters' actions? In analyzing the characters' faces and emotions, what does the illustrator do for her reader? Why would the characters believe that wisdom could be found in a tangible item? Why does the author pay close attention to nature in her book? Describe the penny that is found in the well. How does Jenny react to it compared to the others?	How did Jenny's age and innocence play a role in her character? When comparing the other characters and the wise woman, what role does impatience play in losing sight of happiness? Where in the text can you find evidence of the impact of impatience on the characters' actions and emotions? Why does the wise woman comment on the nature around her? What is the value in enjoying the untouched nature? How does that nature reflect the character of Jenny? In what ways might the tarnished penny symbolize the characters? How will curiosity, patience, and wonder provide wisdom and happiness?

Continued

Table 17.1. Continued

	What is the wise woman's message for Jenny? How does the wise woman's approach to savoring lead to her happiness?	How might this approach to savoring life have led to Jenny's happiness?
Formative Performance Task	*Formative Performance Task*	*Formative Performance Task*
Students will watch a humorous clip from the movie *What about Bob* in which Bill Murray savors his food. Students will then watch a serious clip on savoring and be given an assignment. Students' inferences will guide their reading of *The Wise Woman and Her Secret*.	Students will share answers to the guiding questions in a Google Document, Pear Deck, Padlet, or similar technological sharing application.	Choosing the product of their choice (written piece, slide presentation, art, shared Padlet, etc.), students will portray ways in which they have savored experiences in their lives. Their experiences being displayed in their product, students will conceptualize the positive experiences and emotions that were produced by their intentional savoring of life around them.
Featured Sources	*Featured Sources*	*Featured Sources*
What about Bob? https://www.youtube.com/watch?v=KvVKFCP5cCA *Savoring* https://www.youtube.com/watch?v=qJMqPWhUYxQ	*The Wise Woman and Her Secret* by Eve Merriam Illustrator: Linda Graves	Google Documents, Google Slides, Google Drawings, Padlet, or any digital canvas for presentation

Summative Performance Task	**Argument**	Students will create a final product based on their choice portraying the ways in which savoring life led to their own positive experiences and emotions.
	Extension	After reading and unpacking *The Wise Woman and Her Secret*, students will research different texts that highlight characters who find happiness through patience, curiosity, and wonder. Students will analyze and document the connections those characters have when compared to the wise woman.
Taking Informed Action (Enrichment)		Using a video creation program such as iMovie or WeVideo, students will perform an original script for a happiness movie trailer through creative performance and display the art of savoring.

STAGING THE LESSON

After students watch a humorous clip from the movie *What about Bob?* in which Bill Murray obnoxiously enjoys a meal savoring every bite. This will lead the class into a discussion of savoring and their eating habits.

A more serious film clip will follow in which the idea and practice of mindful savoring is taught to students. Students will then take a directed walk outside the school and be provided with a quiet time to savor something that may have been missed in daily trips around the playground. Without speaking, students will return and write in their journal the feelings and observations on the experience of heightened awareness.

Students will do the homework that night to savor something that is truly impactful and write in their journal the questions on savoring that are contained on the clip. Students will be asked to spend a focused time truly savoring this truly enjoyable experience for a week.

Beginning the lesson the next day, the teacher will engage students in questioning the beauty of mindfulness and the power that can be achieved through savoring the moment. This conversation will transition into discussion and activities that lead directly into the read-aloud.

THE READ-ALOUD: STORIES THAT STICK

The students are now ready to engage in the read-aloud exploring the story in whatever format that the teacher chooses to share the story. Questions before, during, and after the reading are on the template and are provided merely as suggestions.

It is the belief of the authors that questions used to drive the reading are best created by the individual classroom teacher as part of the teachable moments that make read-aloud experiences come to life. More than likely, the suggestions will get you started and follow-up questions will arise in response to students' reactions.

SUMMATIVE PERFORMANCE TASK

Extension

Students will be asked to share the story and the idea of savoring with parents. With parents or guardians if possible, the family will share experiences that they savor. Students will create a bulletin board with illustrations of all the differing things that are savored by both the children and their parents.

In order to assess students' understanding of the essential question, the summative performance task prompts students to create a final product of their choosing to demonstrate how moments of their own savoring led to their positive experiences and emotions. The teacher should provide choices for students to direct them in the precise direction.

Students may opt to reflect in a written piece, create a digital portfolio such as Seesaw, create a short film trailer, or create artwork to depict connections. Important in this process is the students' ability to make connections (and create them) between personal life and the themes found in *A Wise Woman and Her Secret*. In the creation, students should be prompted to reference specific evidence from the text. This strategy will assist students in creating the connection between text and self.

Once students are able to construct clear text-to-self connections and creatively depict them through the process and in the selected medium, they will be directed to complete short research and discovery activities to make connections to other texts and characters. For this task, students will read different texts that highlight characters who discover happiness through patience, curiosity, and wonder.

After reading the various texts, students will develop a piece of writing that will capture the connections between the wise woman and the characters in the other texts. Teachers should prompt students to develop a clear thesis, include textual evidence from chosen texts, and clearly present the connections between the mindsets of all characters. The process and product for this activity should be differentiated based on students' needs.

For both tasks, before students begin to work on their product of choice to highlight their understanding, they should review a rubric that will be used for evaluation purposes. Teachers are recommended to use rubrics that are consistent with past assignments and expectations. As part of the evaluation process, students' reflections should play an important role in the assessment. Teachers may want to use the rubrics often throughout the process to chart and document students' growth.

TAKING INFORMED ACTION

Using a video creation program such as iMovie or WeVideo, students will perform an original script for a happiness movie trailer and, through creative performance, display the art of savoring. To provide mentor texts for students, teachers are recommended to show students sample movie trailers, discuss the elements of effective trailers, analyze approaches when creating a trailer for an intended audience, and brainstorm the impact that color, song, lighting, mood, and language have on an audience's impression of a movie trailer.

After watching the sample trailers and discussing the effective elements of trailer design, students will begin to collaborate on an original script. Students should work collaboratively in the creation of the script. Using a collaborative document such as a Google document, students will be able to share ideas and assist each other with the pieces of the script.

Once the teacher has approved the script, students may begin the performance aspect. Using video creation software or digital applications, students will be able to document their learning and perform their scripts. If available, a green screen and a green screen application can be utilized to create any background of the students choosing that matches the type of happiness that is performed. To connect to *The Wise Woman and Her Secret*, students should be prompted to demonstrate the experience of savoring. This is a key piece in students' projects.

Chapter 18

Choosing Happiness

The Power of Optimism

It's Okay to Make Mistakes by Todd Parr

HOW THIS BOOK CONNECTS TO POSITIVE PSYCHOLOGY RESEARCH ON HAPPINESS

It's Okay to Make Mistakes is a book that reveals to children the essence of optimism and provides a fitting conclusion to the research that has been shared. The father of positive psychology, Martin Seligman, has devoted his life to unlocking the mystery of how we can live more fulfilling and happy lives. No research more girds that pursuit than Seligman's research on well-being and optimism.

The key ideas in this chapter build on the research shared in the previous two chapters by Sonja Lyubomirsky. Lyubomirsky contends that happiness is not as much what happens to individuals, but how individuals react to what happens. Seligman expands this tenet providing a clear description of the differing worldviews that are the heart of our reactions to setbacks in life. Seligman's research defines and explores the opposite reactions that explain the views of optimists and pessimists on the world.

Optimists see mistakes as a temporary setbacks and not permanent conditions. A student who fails a math test on fractions with an optimistic attitude might exhibit a reaction, expressing the belief that harder work on the topic is required so the material can be learned for the final. A pessimist would see the failure as permanent and traced to a pervasive condition of not being able to do mathematics at all.

An optimist would see the failure as specific and not pervasive. The student failing the test on fractions might be heard to say, "I really can't do fractions!" and not, "I really can't do math!" The pessimist would expand the failure to all of mathematics. This broad view of the failure makes the situation seem hopeless to the pessimist.

The optimist would see the setback on the fraction test as within his control to fix, whereas the pessimist would see the situation as out of his locus of control. The optimist might echo the belief that all of us can fail a test, and believe the next test will bring better results with more effort. The conversation in the head of the pessimist in this same predicament would be very different. This conversation might resound with pervasive, permanent, and uncontrollable belief that doing well in mathematics, ever, is not a possibility.

It's Okay to Make Mistakes presents the case for optimism sharing on each page how mistakes, which could be viewed as negative events, can lead to positive outcomes. This story shares with the readers the possibility that positive results may arise unexpectedly from negative events.

Lyubomirsky's *Myths of Happiness* makes the same case in research that what we believe are negative events can often result in positive events in our lives. Her studies reveal that divorces, the loss of a job, getting older, and even being diagnosed with cancer can have positive outcomes if viewed as opportunities for growth.

Barbara Frederickson shares the idea that we are in control of our own positivity in her landmark research on positive emotions shared in *positivity*. Frederickson's research on opening one's minds to a broader, more open view on life's events opens every individual to the possibility of leading a more creative and more happy life. Her theory, known as *Broaden and Build*, suggests individuals broaden views on the positivity that surrounds them to build new skills, relationships, and new ways of being.

It's Okay to Make Mistakes offers a fitting conclusion to the selected stories as the book brings the research full circle by tying together the opening story on growth mindset, where the students were asked if mistakes were good or bad, to an even richer connection between a growth mindset, optimism, and, ultimately, happiness. Students can, in this final chapter, understand the overlapping and interconnected nature of how an individual thinks and how these thoughts make that individual feel and, ultimately, act.

The hope is that the research revealed in this process leads to more than good grades. The hope is that the understandings can help children discover a more fulfilling and happier life. In learning the vocabulary and lesson driving positive psychology, it is hoped that children will be armed with the tools to understand the thoughts that define their views on life and their own well-being.

More detailed information on happiness research is available for teachers and parents in the reference section in Chapter 20 of this book. These shared sources on happiness include YouTube presentations, books that can change your life, and scholarly research from which the positive psychology supporting the chapter has been derived.

Lesson Design: *It's Okay to Make Mistakes*
Kelly Marzocchi, Caitlin Verity, and Megan Votke

Table 18.1. The Power of Optimism: *It's Okay to Make Mistakes* **by Todd Parr**

Compelling Question	Can optimism be learned?
Common Core Standards	• CCSS.ELA-LITERACY.CCRA.R.2 • CCSS.ELA-LITERACY.CCRA.SL.1 • CCSS.ELA-LITERACY.CCRA.W.1 • NCSS—Theme 4: Individual Development and Identity • NCSS Inquiry Arc—Dimension 4
Staging the Question	Students will analyze a glass of water. They will think about the question, *Do you think this glass of water is half empty or half full?* Students will record their answers on Post-its. The teacher will divide the class into two groups—half full and half empty—for a debate.

Supporting Question 1 (Before reading) What is the difference between optimism and pessimism?	*Supporting Question 2 (During reading)* Why does the book It's Okay to Make Mistakes *feel it is OK to make mistakes?*	*Supporting Question 3 (After reading)* How can we maintain an optimistic attitude toward the problems in our lives?
Do you think this glass of water is half empty or half full? Which perspective reflects a positive point of view? Which perspective reflects a negative point of view? What are characteristics of an optimistic person? What are characteristics of a pessimistic person? Do you typically react to situations with an optimistic or pessimistic outlook? **Higher-Level Questions:** How do you think this shapes your character? Can you think of someone in your life that typically reacts with the opposite outlook as you? How does someone develop character traits? Did someone teach you these character traits? Are there people in your lives that serve as role models who have these character traits?	Have you ever been hesitant to try something new? After you tried it, how did your feelings change? Have you ever wanted to ask a question in class but you were afraid to? How many of you asked the question? What happened after you took that risk? Have you ever done something that is unique to your character? What's an "uh-oh" moment and how can you learn from it? Take a minute to write down your mistake. What was your reaction?	Did anyone notice a specific pattern the author used while writing his book? What was similar about the pages on the right-hand side of the book in comparison to the left-hand side of the book? Was the point of view of the characters throughout the book, more optimistic or pessimistic?

Continued

Table 18.1. Continued

Formative Performance Task	*Formative Performance Task*	*Formative Performance Task*
Students will work with their cooperative group in preparation for a debate where they will collaborate and jot down notes to justify their thinking.	As the teacher poses the questions, students will conduct a "Turn and Talk" or engage in a class discussion.	Students will complete sentence frames modeled after the pattern in Parr's book. This will allow for them to identify a situation that they have been challenged with and to show both an optimistic and a pessimistic mindset.
Featured Sources	*Featured Sources*	*Featured Sources*
A glass of water filled to the halfway mark	*It's Okay to Make Mistakes* by Todd Parr	Sentence Frames

Summative Performance Task	**Argument**	Students will write a reflective piece in their writer's notebook to justify why it is important to have an optimistic outlook and answer the compelling question: Can optimism be learned?
	Extension	Students will share what they know about the words "optimism" and "pessimism." They will ask their parents to tell them about a time that they felt challenged and share the path that they took. Students will then share the challenges with their parents. Students may begin to explore the area of mindfulness with the teacher.
Taking Informed Action (Enrichment)		Students will create a school-wide binder in which they will compile behavior reflection forms to share with their peers. These forms will serve as a resource for the school community when they feel they are in need of support and guidance. Student representatives called "optimistic agents" will be in place to act as leaders in the optimism movement. There is also a possibility of beginning a class meditation practice based on teacher inclination and support.

STAGING THE LESSON

The primary focus of this lesson is for students to develop an understanding of optimism and whether or not it can be a learned way of thinking. An individual's mindset is often influenced by his or her life experiences through the concept of nature versus nurture. In today's society, students within classrooms come from various backgrounds, including diverse socioeconomic status, race, religion, and gender.

Although educators lack the ability to control an individual's innate behaviors, teachers can do their best to cultivate an environment that will allow students to develop optimistic views on failure. Teachers should encourage an optimistic mindset and use relatable situations that may occur in all aspects of a child's life to mold their mindset in a positive way.

For example, teaching students to "fail well" in situations including, but not limited to, losing a sporting event, failing a test, the fear of taking risks, and resolving peer conflicts gives opportunities for teachable moments. It is essential to provide these young minds with strategies to recognize and identify the importance of optimism, and use the research that failure is not permanent, pervasive, and innate.

As students begin to analyze individual experiences, they should develop a deeper metacognitive awareness and begin to further understand the reasoning behind a point of view, whether it is optimistic or pessimistic. The ultimate goal is for students to embrace a more optimistic approach to life, while internalizing the benefits.

To begin the lesson, the teacher will have students analyze a glass of water. The teacher will pose the question, *Do you think this glass of water is half empty or half full?* Students will record their answer on a Post-it, which will prompt the teacher to divide the class into two groups: half full versus half empty. Students will collaborate with their group in preparation for a debate and jot down notes in support of a position.

Teachers should use their discretion to determine the appropriate length of time allotted for this activity. Students may need additional prompting throughout this process based on previous exposure to conversational skills. The teacher will end the debate by stating that both sides are correct in the way the glass of water was viewed, but each side from a different perspective.

This will spearhead a class discussion that will lead to an explanation on the distinguishing factors between an optimistic and pessimistic perception covered in connection to positive psychology preface to this chapter. The teacher will explore the possible ways that one might look at missing a shot in basketball, detailing the self-talk of an optimist and a pessimist.

THE READ-ALOUD: STORIES THAT STICK

The students are now ready to engage in the read-aloud exploring the story in whatever format that the teacher chooses to share the story. Questions before, during, and after the reading are on the template and are provided merely as suggestions.

It is the belief of the authors that questions used to drive the reading are best created by the individual classroom teacher as part of the teachable moments that make read-aloud experiences come to life. More than likely, the suggestions will get you started and follow-up questions will arise in response to students' reactions.

SUMMATIVE PERFORMANCE TASK

Argument

After the reading, students will write a reflective piece in a writer's notebook to share a time in their lives when having an optimistic outlook on life made all the difference. In addition, the children should be able to answer the compelling question, *Can optimism be learned?* This will provide an opportunity for all students to solidify their understanding of optimism and apply this to everyday emotional situations, whether individually or as a peer mentor.

Extension

As an extension, students will share what they have learned about optimism and pessimism with their families. They will then ask a person in the family to share with them about a time that things did not go well and the path taken.

Students will then share the challenges their families took with their classmates to recognize that regardless of their background, all have experienced "uh oh" and "oh no" moments in life. The difference is often in how individuals react to those moments. Students and their parents may wish to visit Barbara Frederickson's website on mindfulness meditation, Loving Kindness Meditation (http://positivityresonance.com/meditations.html), to share in mindfulness meditation.

TAKING INFORMED ACTION

Although this inquiry-based lesson is designed to be utilized within the classroom, it should be expanded to become a school-wide movement. In order to promote optimism for all learners, teachers should be encouraged to collaborate with their grade levels to develop a system that will intrinsically motivate students to become independent thinkers, in regard to their emotional state.

As a means of instilling this virtue, students will complete a reflective form, as situations arise, that will allow them to share individual stories of optimism that live on after the read-aloud. Forms should be used in accordance with the appropriate grade levels to ensure that the children can successfully complete the task.

Regardless of their age, each form should outline the situation that occurred, explaining inner thought processes by describing the feelings before choosing the optimistic path, and a reflection on the expressed feelings after. In addition, the form should include the benefits and strategies that support the chosen path.

Each grade level will be responsible for producing a binder that will compile instances where students faced a challenge that threatened optimism. Students will be provided with the opportunity to add to the binder as frequently as needed, deciding whether or not to disclose their identity or remain anonymous.

To maintain the usefulness of this binder, it is essential to institute student representatives to act as "optimistic agents," who will be responsible for organizing and categorizing the binder so that it is easily accessible and effectively utilized. Examples of categories can include, but are not limited to, family, friendship, school, and extracurricular activities.

The purpose of this ongoing behavioral documentation is to collect data that will assist students in self-motivated peer support and guidance. The optimal vision is to influence our youngsters to become proactive members of society and, in turn, transcend this movement into the school community.

Through self-discovery, students will come to the realization that they are the stakeholders within their lives and the power to define their destiny is in their hands. The essence of this book will prove that "it's okay to make mistakes," as mistakes can foster growth by forcing us to discover new paths.

Depending on the inclination of the teacher, to support the idea of controlling one's thoughts in reaction to experience, the teacher may wish to investigate the practice of meditation. With parental support, students may practice the mindfulness on a daily or weekly basis. An ideal and easy way to begin is to employ the Loving Kindness Meditation practiced on Barbara

Pessimistic Reaction	It's okay to _____.	Optimistic Reaction
Write about reaction that could have happened.		Write about reaction that did happen.
	Draw scene of what happened that could have been negative.	

Figure 18.1. Student Optimism

Frederickson's mindfulness website (http://positivityresonance.com/meditations.html).

This direction can be pursued only with a passionate and knowledgeable principal, a supportive administration, and parental permission. There are now school-wide programs that employ mindfulness meditation that have resulted in researched improvement in student focus, academic performance, and discipline. The practice may have a snowball effect on the entire school.

Part III

THE BEGINNING, NOT THE END

Chapter 19

Building Culture

This Book Is the Beginning, Not the End

There is little chance that reading each selected story and teaching the lesson built on that reading will magically transform the character of each child. The lessons merely internalize a vocabulary and an understanding of the positive psychology constructs. If the lessons are to involve changes in belief and behavior, this vocabulary and its beliefs must help define a culture that takes hold in the child and the classroom.

Pete Carroll of the Seahawks took offense to Duckworth's call to arms exhorting teachers to find measures to grow grit, but suggesting that science was not in a place that could be sure if that was even possible. What Carroll found most offensive in Duckworth's challenge was the contention there was no idea on how to instill grit in children. Carroll's contention was that the personal mission that defines his coaching revolves around building cultures of grit in his football teams. The Seattle Seahawks football team is the embodiment of a culture constructed around a culture of grit.

Carroll contends that his coaching has the goal of competing every day, which he describes as *striving together* in his book *Win Forever*. Since their first phone call, Duckworth and Carroll have formed a mutual admiration society and learned much from their unique collaboration.

The idea that we can create cultures of grit in schools is the intriguing possibility that arises from this eclectic partnership. One can only imagine our students and our schools adopting a motto of *striving together*. This thinking that grit is not created in lessons but can be created by culture is also the theory driving Paul Tough's new book, *Helping Children Succeed*. Tough maintains that the hard way to develop grit is for an individual to do it on his or her own, but the easy way to build it is to join a team or organization where grit is the prevailing character trait that defines the culture of the organization.

What Tough's work implies for teachers and schools should be obvious. Teachers, parents, and schools must not simply teach about grit, but we must seek to create cultures of grit. Tough suggests that some of the strongest teachers of grit function without ever using the positive psychology vocabulary, but they instill grit by demanding and expecting high expectations of their constituents.

Although Tough describes paragons of cultural grit as often oblivious to the vocabulary, those wishing to create cultural shifts might best begin with a common core of vocabulary and understandings shared in this book. To facilitate cultural change of high expectations and greater effort, students must first internalize those definitions and the language must become the working vocabulary of the classroom.

Before assimilating and adopting a culture of grit, students must first know the why behind the adoption of greater expectations. There is no disagreement that the real work for teachers, students, and parents is to make these new internalized beliefs the philosophy of student actions in the classroom and supported by parents at home. The stories that are shared in this work may need to be reviewed and revisited over time to reinforce the learning.

The process of internalizing the "why" in students that is shared in the positive psychology research may provide the motivation that students need to build a new culture of greater effort. In *Every Book Is a Social Studies Book: How to Meet Standards with Picture Books, K-6*, Libresco and Balantic (2009) have created a superior text on how to teach the lessons of history through trade books. Their underlying goal is that when students and teachers begin to see the lessons of history as they are in life, ongoing and everywhere around them, they will begin to live as truly informed citizens.

In the same way that history is all around us if we only look, it is the dream of this work that students begin to see the lessons of positive psychology present in every domain and context of life. Teachers are not limited to literature to find powerful positive psychology connections. Hopefully, teachers will be inspired to create personal connections to character in subject disciplines, as were social studies methods students at Molloy College. There are no limits to the connections that surround us.

Examine the website (www.edu509class.weebly.com); this is a unit plan structured to teach women's rights by viewing the movement as products of growth mindset and grit. In fall 2016, social studies methods students at Molloy College created a website, behindthecurtainsofhistory.weebly.com, which views history at various grade levels as history of individuals affected by growth mindset, hope, grit, and character strengths. Each of their lesson segments is built off a story featured in this text.

These lessons use the building blocks of positive psychology to analyze events in history, but it is a short leap to imagine teachers creating lessons in literature or science. Building the culture will result only when the beliefs, actions, and standards are adopted by all in the learning community. Your own possible connections are probably now percolating as you read and investigate those shared here. Live this curriculum and create your own.

There may be no place where growth mindset and the ability to fail well are more essential than in the initiatives seeking to introduce elementary students to greater levels of complexity in science, technology, engineering, arts, and mathematics. Cultures will have to be developed that strengthen the resolve students will need to meet these challenges. Students will need to better accept failure and develop the resilience and effort needed to meet more of these demanding challenges.

This book offers its own call to arms to the reader to create personal pathway directions and connections to positive psychology. Efforts and insights can be shared with the authors at:

E-mail: ksheehan1@molloy.edu and MrsJessicaRyan@gmail.com
Twitter handles: @sheehank11 and @MrsJessicaRyan

The ultimate goal is that after repeated curricular connections to positive psychology traits, students will begin to see examples of failing well, effort, hope, grit, and strengths shaping every aspect of experience.

Powerful experiences not only bring to life the lessons in positive psychology but also define the quality of our daily lives. These lessons are not from a text or curriculum, but are the experiences that shape the direction of our lives and our ultimate happiness. The greatest hope of this book is that it truly is the beginning and not the end, for all, for students, but also for you, the teacher.

The beginning is that we use this book to form a community based on creating cultures of hope and grit. The end is that students begin to be shaped by those cultures defined by the character traits that they derive from these stories and lessons. The grit that Duckworth calls for will not arise from a lesson and cannot be taught. It is the triumph over adversity that must be lived.

The groundbreaking work of *Project Zero* shares truly innovative strategies for having students explore the inner workings of their cognitive processes across disciplines. This program urges that teachers *and schools* establish routines for making thinking visible in regard to understanding, creativity, fairness, and truth. The central unifying idea is that routines structure the process of thinking and make the act of metacognition a habit.

The final dream of this book is that schools will one day establish the time for a routine that allows children to make their thinking about their beliefs about self, goals, strengths, and happiness visible. Those strategies and routines will unleash thinking that has the power to truly inspire hope, grit, and happiness in every child. Consider this book the beginning, and not the end, of that dream.

Chapter 20

Deeper Knowledge

Resources for Teachers and Parents for Learning More about Mindset, Hope, Grit, Strengths, and Happiness

RESOURCES FOR LEARNING MORE ABOUT MINDSET

YouTube Mindset Videos

1. In this video, Dr. Carol Dweck discusses the definition of happiness and its connection to mindset. Dr. Dweck explains the differences and consequences of having a fixed mindset and having a growth mindset. Research indicates that those with a growth mindset do better in many aspects of life, but especially in school. She discusses mindset differences between age and grade levels (26:31).
   https://www.youtube.com/watch?v=QGvR_0mNpWM
   Dweck, C. (2013, October 20). Mindset—the new psychology of success at happiness & its causes 2013. [Video file.] Retrieved from http://www.youtube.com/watch?v=qaeFnxSfSC4

2. This video provides a humorous look into the thought process students may go through before answering a difficult question in class. The video provides a window on the reasons many students do not answer in class (0:55).
   https://www.youtube.com/watch?v=UNAMrZr9OWY
   GoStrengths Online (2012, June 6). Fixed vs. growth mindsets in children. [Video file.] Retrieved from https://www.youtube.com/watch?v=UNAMrZr9OWY

3. This video presents the case that a growth mindset is a way we can train our brains to become smarter (2:31).
   https://www.youtube.com/watch?v=ElVUqv0v1EE
   Infobundl (2014, June 2). Growth mindset video. [Video file.] Retrieved from https://www.youtube.com/watch?v=ElVUqv0v1EE

4. Dr. Carol Dweck discusses the power of "yet" and teaching students to respond "not yet" can lay the foundation for a growth mindset. Dweck points out that students should be focused on the power of "yet," as a way to see failure as a necessary step to a more positive future. Dr. Dweck explains how we can get our students to this point of connecting now and "yet" (9:37).
https://www.youtube.com/watch?v=hiiEeMN7vbQ
Dweck, C. (2014, October 9). Developing a growth mindset. [Video file.] Retrieved from https://www.youtube.com/watch?v=hiiEeMN7vbQ

5. Child prodigy Adora Svitak promotes "childish" thinking including bold ideas, wild creativity, and especially optimism. This is a great video to help parents realize that children have innate gifts and need not be driven toward limiting performance goals (10:44).
https://www.youtube.com/watch?v=V-bjOJzB7LY
Svitak, A. (2010, April 2). What adults can learn from kids. [Video file.] Retrieved from https://www.youtube.com/watch?v=V-bjOJzB7LY

"Must Read" Mindset Books That Can Change Your Life

Dweck, C. W. (2012). *Mindset: The new psychology of success*. New York: Ballantine.

Mraz, K. & Hertz, C. (2015). *A mindset for learning: Teaching the traits of joyful, independent growth.* New York: Heinemann.

Ricci, M. C. (2013). *Mindsets in the classroom: Building a culture of success and student achievement in schools.* New York: Prufrock Press.

Social Media

Twitter Handles:
@CarolIdweck
@Growthmindset1

Facebook Page:

https://www.facebook.com/CarolDweckAuthor/

Mindset Websites:

Mindsetonline.com
Brainology
http://www.mindsetworks.com/
Edutopia
http://www.edutopia.org/article/growth-mindset-resources

The King and His Carpenters, Farr and (Farr & Tone, 1998)
http://users.metu.edu.tr/eryilmaz/Courses/SCE410/King_Carpenter.htm

Mindset Website Test

http://www.edpartnerships.org/sites/default/files/events/2016/02/Mind
set%20Quiz.pdf

Scholarly Articles on the Key Mindset Research

Dweck, C. S. (2000). *Self-theories: Their role in motivation, personality, and development.* New York: Routledge.
Dweck, C. S. (2012). *Mindset: How you can fulfill your potential.* New York: Random House.
Yeager, D. S., & Dweck, C. S. (2012). Mindsets that promote resilience: When students believe that personal characteristics can be developed. *Educational Psychologist, 47*(4), 302–314.

RESOURCES FOR LEARNING MORE ABOUT HOPE

YouTube Hope Videos

1. Shane Lopez 40 minutes on Hope
   Shane Lopez discusses the importance of hope and its significance in goal attainment. Lopez proposes that students, and all of us, are predominately in a state of thinking about their future. Students' focused and directed thinking about what they want in life increases hope. The video provides great detail on the importance of hope in living a fulfilling life (22:01).
   https://www.youtube.com/watch?v=AXBEoTepQHQ
   Lopez, S. J. (2014, January 9). Hope is a Strategy. [Video file.] Retrieved from https://www.youtube.com/watch?v=AXBEoTepQHQ

2. Dr. Shane Lopez, as the senior scientist at Gallup, discusses hope and why individuals need to be hopeful. Lopez addresses the differences between hoping and wishing, and strategies to harness the power of hope (9:39).
   https://www.youtube.com/watch?v=Bka3sI5_WZ4
   Lopez, S. J. (2013, May 7). Interview with Dr. Shane Lopez. [Video file.]. Retrieved from https://www.youtube.com/watch?v=Bka3sI5_WZ4

3. In an interview with Lisa Buxbaum, Dr. Shane Lopez discusses the impacts hope has on health. Lopez discusses why it is vital to keep the vision of the future of our dreams alive and provides strategies on how to model hope for others (13:44).

https://www.youtube.com/watch?v=UN3ZvG-Z0vg
Soaring Words. (2013, August 6). Making hope happen with Shane Lopez. [Video file.] Retrieved from https://www.youtube.com/watch?v=UN3Z vG-Z0vg

4. Dr. Shane Lopez briefly explains why hope is important for student success as well as a predictor of college readiness (1:09).
https://www.youtube.com/watch?v=P6QYUp57EwI
Battelle for Kids. (2015, February 27). Hope matters for student success. [Video file.] Retrieved from https://www.youtube.com/watch?v= P6QYUp57EwI

"Must Read" Hope Books That Can Change Your Life

Lopez, S.J. (2013). *Making hope happen: Create the future you want for yourself and others*. New York: Simon and Shuster.

McDermott, D., & Snyder, C.R. (1999). *Making hope happen: A workbook for turning possibilities into realities*. Oakland, CA: New Harbingers Publications.

Pearpoint, J., O'Brien, J., & Forest, M. (1993). PATH: A workbook for planning positive possible futures. *Planning alternative tomorrows with hope for schools, organizations, business, families*. Toronto: Inclusion Press.

Social Media

Twitter Handle:
@hopemonger
Facebook Page:
https://www.facebook.com/pages/Shane-J-Lopez/557581220940888?fref=ts

Hope Website:

http://hopemonger.com/

Hope Website Test:

https://molloy.instructure.com/courses/4083/files/72629/download? download_frd=1

Scholarly Articles on Key Hope Research

Lopez, S.J. (2011). Making ripples of hope. *Educational Horizons, 89*(4), 9–13.

Lopez, S.J. (2012). The how of hope. *Phi Delta Kappan, 93*(8), 72–73.

Lopez, S.J. (2013). Making hope happen in the classroom. *Phi Delta Kappan, 95*(2), 72–73.

Oaklander, M (2015) The science of bouncing back. *Time* magazine. http://time.com/3892044/the-science-of-bouncing-back/

Snyder, C.R. (Ed). (2000). *The handbook of hope*. San Diego, CA: Academic Press.

Snyder, C.R. (2002). Hope theory: Rainbows in the mind. *Psychological Inquiry, 13*(4), 249–275.

Snyder, C.R., Harris, C., Anderson, J.R., Holleran, S.A., Irving, L.M., Sigmund, S., Harney, P. (1991). The will and the ways: Development and validation of the individual-differences measure of hope. *Journal of Personality and Social Psychology, 60*, 570–585.

RESOURCES FOR LEARNING MORE ABOUT GRIT

YouTube Grit Videos

1. Duckworth's Legendary TED talk that introduces her research on grit and the applications of grit theory as a key factor in success at West Point, in Ivy League schools and at the National Spelling Bee (18:38).
   http://www.youtube.com/watch?v=qaeFnxSfSC4
   Duckworth, A.L. (2009, October 18). True grit: Can perseverance be taught? [Video file.] Retrieved from http://www.youtube.com/watch?v=qaeFnxSfSC4

2. Duckworth's captivating follow-up TED talk that applies grit research to teaching and poses the challenge of how we teach kids to be grittier. This presentation makes clear the connection between grit and the mindset research of Carol Dweck (6:12).
   http://www.ted.com/talks/angela_lee_duckworth_the_key_to_success_grit.hml.
   Duckworth, A.L. (2013, May 9). The key to success: Grit? [Video file.] Retrieved from http://www.ted.com/talk/angela_lee_duckworth_the_key_to_success_grit.hml.

3. Amy Lyona, a fifth-grade teacher in Vermont, adjusts her curriculum to teach grit and create grittier students. Applying Duckworth's definition and understandings about grit, this video offers teachers concrete pathways to teaching grit in the classroom (6:20).
   https://www.youtube.com/watch?v=F0qrtsYg6kI
   Edutopia (2014, April 29). Teaching grit cultivates resilience and perseverance. [Video file.] Retrieved from https://www.youtube.com/watch?v=F0qrtsYg6kI

4. Amy Lyon shares one strategy for teaching grit, *the Perseverance Walk*, a project in which students are asked to interview a person who has lived a life with grit (2:42).

https://www.youtube.com/watch?v=F6BZ-boSKts
Edutopia (2014, April 29). Grit curriculum lesson: Perseverance walk. [Video file.] Retrieved from https://www.youtube.com/watch?v=F6BZ-boSKt

5. Pete Carroll and Angela Duckworth discuss the culture of grit that defines the Seattle Seahawks football team. In doing so, the researcher and coach collaborate and find common ground on the topic of how to build grit.
   http://www.fieldgulls.com/2016/5/20/11724788/pete-carroll-and-dr-angela-duckworth-on-the-seahawks-grit
   Field Gulls (2016, May 20). Pete Carroll and Dr. Angela Duckworth on the Seahawks' grit. [Video file.] Retrieved from http://www.fieldgulls.com/2016/5/20/11724788/pete-carroll-and-dr-angela-duckworth-on-the-seahawks-grit

"Must Read" Grit Books That Can Change Your Life

Duckworth, A. (2016). *Grit: Passion and perseverance*. New York: Simon and Shuster.
Pink, D. H. (2011). *Drive: The surprising truth about what motivates us*. New York: Penguin.
Solarz, P (2015). *Learn like a pirate: Empower your students to collaborate, lead and succeed*. San Diego, CA. Dave Burgess Consulting Inc.
Tough, P. (2012). *How children succeed: Grit, curiosity and the hidden power of character*. New York: Houghton Mifflin.
Tough, P. (2016). *Helping children succeed: What works and why*. New York: Houghton Mifflin.

Social Media

Twitter Handle:
@angeladuckw
Facebook Page:
https://www.facebook.com/angeladuckworthgrit/?fref=nf

Grit Websites:

http://angeladuckworth.com/
http://LearnLikeAPirate.com
http://geniushour.com

Grit Website Test:

http://www.sas.upenn.edu/~duckwort/images/8-item%20Grit%20Scale_Child%20Adapted%20Version_4.pdf

Scholarly Articles on the Key Grit Research

Duckworth, A. L., Grant, H., Loew, B., Oettingen, G., & Gollwitzer, P.M. (2011). Self-regulation strategies improve self-discipline in adolescents: Benefits of mental contrasting and implementation intentions. *Educational Psychology, 31*(1), 17–26.

Duckworth, A. L., Peterson, C., Matthews, M. D., & Kelly, D. R. (2007). Grit: Perseverance and passion for long-term goals. *Journal of Personality and Social Psychology, 92*(6), 1087–1101.

Duckworth, A. L., & Quinn, P. D. (2009) Development and validation of the short grit scale. *Journal of Personality Assessment, 91*(2), 166–174.

Duckworth, A. L., & Seligman, M. E. P. (2005). Self-discipline outdoes IQ in predicting academic performance of adolescents. *American Psychological Society, 16*(12), 939–944.

Tough, P. (2011, September 18) What if the secret of success is failure? *The New York Times Magazine, 85*, 38–46.

Tough, P. (2014). Who gets to graduate. *The New York Times* https://www.nytimes.com/2014/05/18/magazine/who-gets-to-graduate.html, MAY 15, 2014.

RESOURCES FOR LEARNING MORE ABOUT CHARACTER STRENGTHS

YouTube Character Strengths Videos

1. John Yeager shares a series of videos that highlight how to manage strengths and employ the SMART Strengths program.
   https://www.youtube.com/playlist?list=PL1tVv4jP4DvUiWhe mlR-IltW4EUszDe0b
   Smart Strengths (2012, November 14). Smart Strengths with John Yeager. [Video file.] Retrieved from https://www.youtube.com/playlist?list=PL1 tVv4jP4DvUiWhemlR- IltW4EUszDe0b

2. Tom Rath shares his research on our focus on failure rather than strengths in his video on the power of finding your strengths (9:06).
   https://www.youtube.com/watch?v=93anYwdtADs
   Rath, T. (2011, October 22). Find your strengths. [Video file.] Retrieved from https://www.youtube.com/watch?v=93anYwdtADs

3. David Cooperrider shares a brief definition of appreciative inquiry for business, a model that is focused on strengths (3:53).
   https://www.youtube.com/watch?v=3JDfr6KGV-k
   Coopperrider, D. L. (2011, September 1). Appreciative inquiry: A conversation with David Cooperrider. [Video file.] Retrieved from https://www.youtube.com/watch?v=3JDfr6KGV-k

4. David Cooperrider shares his worldview on appreciative inquiry, a model of change for business and politics through shared dreams rather than problems (25:03).
https://www.youtube.com/watch?v=-SoAKaTKAYA
Coopperrider, D. L. (2015, September 25). The power of resilience: David Cooperrider at EDxUNPlaza 2013. [Video file.] Retrieved from https://www.youtube.com/watch?v=-SoAKaTKAYA

5. Martin Seligman ties together the idea of human happiness with the history of positive psychology with his inspiring TED talk on flourishing and the potential for human happiness (23:41).
https://www.youtube.com/watch?v=CbJnPQ9klsQ
Seligman, M. L. (2004, February). The new era of positive psychology. [Video file.] Retrieved from https://www.youtube.com/watch?v=CbJnPQ9klsQ

"Must Read" Character Strengths Books That Can Change Your Life

Cooperrider, D. L., & Whitney, D. (2005). *Appreciative inquiry: A positive revolution in change.* New York: Berrett-Koehler Publishers.
Quinn, R. E. (2010). *Deep change: Discovering the leader within* (Vol. 378). San Francisco, CA: John Wiley & Sons.
Quinn, R. E. (2015). *The positive organization: Breaking free from conventional cultures, constraints, and beliefs.* Berrett-Koehler. Oakland, CA
Rath, T. (2007). STRENGTHFINDER 2.0. New York: GALLUP.
Rath, T. (2013). *Eat, move, sleep. how small changes lead to big changes.* N.A.: Missionday.
Rath, T. (2015). *Are you fully energized? The 3 keys to energizing your work and life.* N.A.: Silicon Guild.
Ritchhart, R., Church, M., & Morrison, K. (2011). *Making thinking visible: How to promote engagement, understanding, and independence for all learners.* San Francisco, CA: John Wiley & Sons.
Yeager, J. M., Fisher, S. W., & Shearon, D. N. (2011). *Smart strengths: A parent-teacher-coach guide to building character, resilience, and relationships in youth.* New York: Kravis Publishing.

Social Media

Twitter Handles:
@SMARTstrengths
@TomcRath
@Dlc6David
Facebook Page:
https://www.facebook.com/authortomrath/

Websites:

http://smartstrengths.com
http://tomrathorg

Tests/Websites:

Find Your Strengths VIA—Virtues in Action
http://www.viacharacter.org/www
Find Your Strengths Clifton Strengths Finder (Tom Rath)
http://www.strengthstest.com/strengths-finder-themes
At My Best Strength Cards
http://atmybest.com/

Scholarly Articles on the Key Character Strengths Research

Cooperrider, D. L., Barrett, F., & Srivastva, S. (1995). Social construction and appreciative inquiry: A journey in organizational theory. *Management and organization: Relational alternatives to individualism*, 157–200.

Csikszentmihalyi, M, (1990) *Flow: The psychology of optimal experience.* New York: Harper Perennials

Park, N., Peterson, C., & Seligman, M. E. (2004). Strengths of character and well-being. *Journal of Social and Clinical Psychology, 23*(5), 603–619.

Peterson, C., & Seligman, M. E. (2004). *Character strengths and virtues: A handbook and classification.* Oxford University Press.

Tough, P. (2016, June). How kids learn resilience. *The Atlantic.* Retrieved http://www.cbsd.org/cms/lib010/PA01916442/Centricity/Domain/2711/How%20Kids%20Learn%20Resilience.pdf

RESOURCES FOR LEARNING MORE ABOUT HAPPINESS

YouTube Happiness Videos

1. Sonja Lyubomirsky's segment on *20/20* presents her research in a manner that shares the findings in a made-for-television style. Lyubomirsky dramatically shares that our life circumstances account for only 10 percent of our happiness (6:57).
   https://www.youtube.com/watch?v=qv6xYmh4Y-w
   Lyubomirsky, A. L. (2008, January 17). Sonja Lyubomirsky on 20/20. [Video file.] Retrieved from https://www.youtube.com/watch?v=qv6xYmh4Y-w

2. Sonja Lyubomirsky's book *The How of Happiness* is reviewed by the philosophersnotes.com life. The big ideas are reviewed in detail (10:00).

https://www.youtube.com/watch?v=aemKdxd-kXY
Johnson, B. (2009, December 2). Review of the how of happiness. [Video file.] Retrieved from https://www.youtube.com/watch?v=aemKdxd-kXY

3. Sonja Lyubomirsky's scholarly presentation of her research to the Seaver Distinguished Lecture Series at Pepperdine University. The presentation is on the science of happiness (1:17:40).
   https://www.youtube.com/watch?v=pIiMc1eO_34
   Lyubomirsky, A. L. (2015, September 25). Sonja Lyubomirsky the Science of Happiness. [Video file.] Retrieved from https://www.youtube.com/watch?v=pIiMc1eO_34

4. The Science of Happiness presents a clever experiment in gratitude, which reveals the power of gratitude by conducting an experiment in which unsuspecting subjects called and expressed gratitude to a key player in their life (7:13).
   https://www.youtube.com/watch?v=oHv6vTKD6lg
   Soul Pancake (2013, July 11). An experiment in gratitude: The Science of Happiness. [Video file.] Retrieved from https://www.youtube.com/watch?v=oHv6vTKD6lg

5. The Greater Good Science Center presents Barbara Frederickson sharing her 3 to 1 Positivity Ratio for happiness. Working with a mathematician, Mariel Losado, Frederickson urges that we measure daily positive experiences and contrasted these with negative emotions, seeking to infuse our life with positive with negative experiences in a 3 to 1 ratio (8:43).
   https://www.youtube.com/watch?v=_hFzxfQpLjM
   Greater Good Science Academy (2011, June 20). Barbara Frederickson: The positivity ratio. [Video file.] Retrieved from https://www.youtube.com/watch?v=_hFzxfQpLjM

"Must Read" Happiness Books That Can Change Your Life

Frederickson, B. L. (2009). *Positivity*. New York: MJF
Frederickson, B. L. (2013). *Love 2.0: How our supreme emotion affects everything we feel, think, do and become.* New York: Hudson Street Press.
Lyubomirsky, S. (2008). *The how of happiness: A scientific approach to getting the life you want.* New York: Penguin.
Lyubomirsky, S. (2013). *The myths of happiness: What should make you happy, but doesn't What shouldn't make you happy but does.* New York: Penguin.
Seligman, M. E. (2012). *Flourish: A visionary new understanding of happiness and well-being.* New York: Simon and Schuster.

Social Media

Twitter Handle:
@slyubomirsky
Facebook Page:
https://www.facebook.com/sonja.lyubomirsky

Websites:

http://fredrickson.socialpsychology.org/
http://sonjalyubomirsky.com/

Tests/Websites:

Find Your Positivity Ratio
http://www.positivityratio.com/single.php
Loving Kindness Meditation/Frederickson
http://positivityresonance.com/meditations.html
University of Pennsylvania's Happiness Tests
https://www.authentichappiness.sas.upenn.edu/testcenter

Scholarly Articles on the Key Happiness Research

Fredrickson, B. L., & Losada, M. F. (2005). Positive affect and the complex dynamics of human flourishing. *American Psychologist, 60*(7), 678.

Lyubomirsky, S. (2001). Why are some people happier than others?: The role of cognitive and motivational processes in well-being. *Social Indicators Research, 56*(3), 239–249.

Lyubomirsky, S., & Lepper, H. S. (1997). A measure of subjective happiness: Preliminary reliability and construct validation. *Social Indicators Research, 46*, 137–115.

Lyubomirsky, S., & Ross, L. (1997). Hedonic consequences of social comparison: A contrast of happy and unhappy people. *Journal of Personality and Social Research, 73*, 1141–1157.

Shen, L., Hsee, C., Zhang, J., & Dai, X. (2011). Belittling can be flattering. *NA-Advances in Consumer Research, 38.*

Postscript

Lessons from the Field: An Insider's View

Jessica Ryan

As with anything you do in the classroom, you have to truly believe in what you are teaching to do an effective job in delivering the information. The concepts presented in this book are simply *good for kids*. We are trying to teach children to be reflective thinkers who can make informed decisions. Students need to be empowered to realize that they steer the course to their very bright futures.

Children's literature provides an even playing field for learners at any grade level to understand the concept. It allows the students to make connections from positive psychology to real life. In a reaction to the strengths lesson using *Going Places*, fourth-grader Mike states, "I think that both Rafael and Maya use their individual abilities to create one big, great idea." The students easily connected the concept of synergy from the story with their experiences during the Marshmallow Challenge (Figure Postscript 2).

To ensure that these lessons were effective, I was able to pilot these positive psychology lessons with feedback from my wonderful colleagues and administrators. In turn, these teachers loved the impact of these lessons so much that they decided to try these lessons out in their own classrooms.

We were able to make adjustments to ensure that these lessons aligned with the proper positive psychology construct, were engaging for students, and were also meaningful. The lessons had to be manageable and realistic for already overburdened classroom teachers. This is not an additional task for teachers, but it intertwined into the content areas.

Where did I find the time? One discovery that we made is that these lessons lend themselves to various content areas. Being that all of them begin using children's literature, the English Language Arts Standards are obvious. However, students use STEAM standards when they are involved in the hands-on formative assessments (see Figures Postscript 1, 2, & 3). Additionally,

Figure Postscript 1.   Iggy Peck Design Challenge

students write to reflect on their firsthand experiences. Character education issues tend to come to the surface when discussing the decisions we make and the people we influence with those decisions.

Another of our findings was that these lessons could not be scripted. The discussions that result from the books that were selected naturally lend themselves to natural and spontaneous conversations on growth mindset, hope, grit, character strengths, and happiness. A skilled teacher will be able to elicit deep learning through questions that arise (from both teachers and students) as the book progresses.

You will need to get parents and guardians involved. One way is by making students have a conversation about the ideas they learned as part of their "home fun." When students are asked what they've learned in school today, so often their response is "Nothing." This area of study provides a strategic plan for parents to talk to their children about their learning and issues that really matter. See Figure Postscript 4 for an example of a home extension in response to the *It's Okay to Make Mistakes* lesson.

Figure Postscript 2.   Cooperative Learning during Marshmallow Challenge

Figure Postscript 3.   Painted Metaphor for Character Strength

<u>It's Okay to Make Mistakes</u> Home Extension

<u>Directions</u>: Share with your parents what you know about "optimism" and "pessimism." Ask your parents about a time they were challenged. What path did they take? Summarize their challenge and path below.

One time my mom was challenged was when my dad was in the war. My brother Dardan was 3 months at the time. My dad was fighting in the Kosovo war. My mom was in America. My mom had to raise my brother for the first few months alone. It was hard on my mom because — she was scared my dad wouldn't be around to see his little boy grow up. She used optimism at this time and told herself everything was going to be okay. She would say it every day to herself and my brother.

Figure Postscript 4.   *It's Okay to Make Mistakes* Home Extension

As you can see, the lessons from this book transcend the classroom walls. The read-aloud experiences provide powerful life lessons that can help guide students with future decision-making. These vital conversations give an opportunity for their parents to be role models in discussing struggles they've had along the way and how to deal with them.

After students have a discussion with their parents about the message of the book, they do an extension activity *together*. Lisa Hoffman, a parent of one of my students, reflected, "I think that doing assignments like these brings a deeper closeness to the parent and child and a better understanding of where a parent is coming from when they give words of encouragement or advice based on their past experiences."

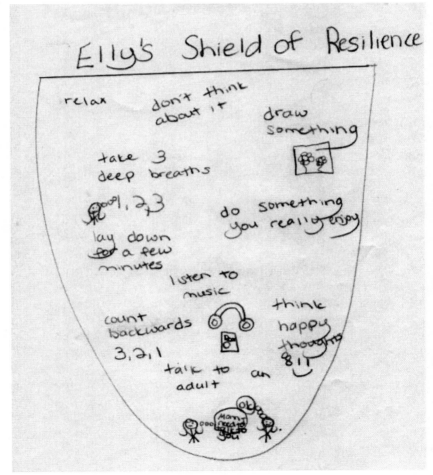

Figure Postscript 5.   Student Shield of Resilience

Figure Postscript 6.   Hope Creator Video

This is the perfect opportunity for parents and children to share their values and dreams. Lisa Hoffman also commented, "My daughter was able to internalize that if she tried really hard and dedicated herself to something she wasn't good at, she would eventually succeed. She knew that this success wasn't going to be instantaneous and that it would be gradual but when she saw the results of her hard work as a grade on a paper, she was so proud of herself."

During a lesson on hope using *Stand Tall, Molly Lou Melon* as the mentor text, students brainstormed how they can deal with hope crushers. Students created "Shields of Resilience" for what to do in the face of adversity. This shield is a resource they can refer to when faced with a difficult situation. As Figure Postscript 5 shows, it is the perfect introduction into problem solving.

Part of the "Taking Informed Action" portion of these lessons requires students to interact in real-world scenarios based on the information they've learned. The QR code (Figure Postscript 6) links to a student-created video on hope creators made by a fourth grader named Allison Hoffman.

The lessons in this book are not a one-shot deal. They have to become part of the culture of your classroom. You will find the lessons on growth mindset and grit come up again and again long after you've closed the read-aloud book. These concepts even creep up when you least expect it; my students have even showed the impact of these concepts during Writers' Workshop within their poetry and personal narratives.

While there are a variety of factors that influence student performance, I had the opportunity to see my students flourish. These positive psychology lessons have impacted my students' mindfulness about their classwork. Their results even translated to improved performances during standardized testing.

It's time to put the theories of growth mindset to the test. So often my students lived the mantra, "I'll be better tomorrow than I am today." By creating hope with a little bit of grit, we are setting our students up for success each day when they leave the classroom.

References

Allen, J. (2015). *No you can't, yes I can*. N.A.: CreateSpace Independent Publishing Platform.

Andreae, G. (2012). *Giraffes can't dance*. New York: Scholastic Books.

Balantic, J., Libresco, A. S., & Kipling, J. C. (2011). *Every book is a social studies book: How to meet standards with picture books, K–6*. Santa Barbara, CA: ABC-CLIO.

Bandura, A. (1977). Self-efficacy: Toward a unifying theory of behavioral change. *Psychological Review, 84*, 191–215.

Beaty, A. (2007). *Iggy peck, architect*. New York: Abrams Books for Young Readers.

Beaty, A. (2013). *Rosie revere, engineer*. New York: Abrams Books for Young Readers.

Catalanotto, P. (2006). *Emily's art*. New York: Atheneum Books for Young Readers.

Cooperrider, D. L., Barrett, F., & Srivastva, S. (1995). Social construction and appreciative inquiry: A journey in organizational theory. In *Management and organization: Relational alternatives to individualism*, Aldershot, UK: Avbury Press, 157–200.

Cooperrider, D. L. & Whitney, D. (2005). *Appreciative inquiry: A positive revolution in change*. New York: Berrett-Koehler Publishers.

Csikszentmihalyi, M., (1990) *Flow: The psychology of optimal experience*. New York: HarperCollins.

Danielson, C. (2014). One to grow on: Teaching like a four star chef. *Educational Leadership,70*(4), 90–91.

Duckworth, A. L. (2009a). (Over and) Beyond high-stakes testing. *American Psychologist, 64*(4), 279–280.

Duckworth, A. L. (2009b, October 18). True grit: Can perseverance be taught? [Video file.] Retrieved from http://www.youtube.com/watch?v=qaeFnxSfSC4

Duckworth, A. L. (2013, May 9). The key to success: Grit? [Video file.] Retrieved from http://www.ted.com/talks/angela_lee_duckworth_the_key_to_success_grit.html

Duckworth, A. L. (2013, August 5). Can perseverance be taught? Big Questions Online. Retrieved from https://www.bigquestionsonline.com/content/can-perseverance-be-taught

Duckworth, A. L. (2016). *Grit: passion and perseverance.* New York: Scribner.

Duckworth, A. L., Grant, H., Loew, B., Oettingen, G., & Gollwitzer, P. M. (2011). Self-regulation strategies improve self-discipline in adolescents: Benefits of mental contrasting and implementation intentions. *Educational Psychology, 31*(1), 17–26.

Duckworth, A. L., Peterson, C., Matthews, M. D., & Kelly, D. R. (2007). Grit: Perseverance and passion for long-term goals. *Journal of Personality and Social Psychology, 92*(6), 1087–1101.

Duckworth, A. L., & Quinn, P. D. (2009). Development and validation of the short grit scale. *Journal of Personality Assessment, 91*(2), 166–174.

Duckworth, A. L., & Seligman, M. E. P. (2005). Self-discipline outdoes IQ in predicting academic performance of adolescents. *American Psychological Society, 16*(12), 939–944.

Dweck, C. S. (2000). *Self-theories: Their role in motivation, personality, and development.* Psychology Press. NY

Dweck, C. S. (2007). The perils and promises of praise. *Kaleidoscope, Contemporary and Classic Readings in Education, 12.* pp 57–61.

Dweck, C. (2012a). *Mindset: How you can fulfill your potential.* Hachette UK. A3 Ballantine Books: New York: New York, 2016.

Dweck, C. W. (2012b). *Mindset: The new psychology of success.* New York: Ballantine

Dweck, C. W., & Molden, C. S. (2005). Self-theories: Their impact on competence motivation and acquisition. In A. J. Elliot & C. S. Dweck (Eds.), *Handbook of competence and motivation* (pp. 122–140). New York: The Guildford Press.

Farr, R. (Ed.). (1993, May). Once upon a time, when there were no tests, children built houses that stood tall and straight . . ." Retrieved from https://archive.org/stream/ERIC_ED364850/ERIC_ED364850_djvu.txt

Farr, R., & Tone, B. (1998). The king and his carpenters. Retrieved from http://users.metu.edu.tr/eryilmaz/Courses/SCE410/King_Carpenter.htm

Frederickson, B. L. (2009). *Positivity.* New York: MJF.

Frederickson, B. L. (2013). *Love 2.0: How our supreme emotion affects everything we feel, think, do and become.* New York: Hudson Street Press.

Fredrickson, B. L., & Losada, M. F. (2005). Positive affect and the complex dynamics of human flourishing. *American Psychologist, 60*(7), 678.

Jordan, D., & Jordan, R. M. (2003). *Salt in his shoes: Michael Jordan in pursuit of a dream.* New York: Simon & Schuster Books for Young Readers.

Lopez, S. J. (2009). *Hope, academic success, and the Gallup student poll: Gallup Student Poll.* Gallup, Inc. Retrieved from www.gallupstudentpoll.com/File/122192

Lopez, S. J. (2011). Making ripples of hope. *Educational Horizons, 89*(4), 9–13.

Lopez, S. J. (2012). Making hope happen in the classroom. *Phi Delta Kappan, 93*(8), 72–73.

Lopez, S. J. (2013a). *Making hope happen: Create the future you want for yourself and others.* New York: Simon and Schuster.

Lopez, S. J. (2013b). Making hope happen in the classroom. *Phi Delta Kappan, 95*(2), 72–73,

Lopez, S. J., Snyder, C. R., Magyar-Moe, J. L., Edwards, L., Pedrotti, J. T. Janowski, K., Turner, J. L. . . & Pressgrove, C. (2004). Strategies for accentuating hope. In

P. A. Linley & S. Joseph (Eds.), *Positive psychology in practice* (pp. 388–404). Hoboken, NJ: John Wiley & Sons.

Lovell, P. (2001). *Stand tall, Molly Lou Melon*. New York: G. P. Putnam's Sons.

Ludwig, T. (2009). *Too perfect*. Berkley, CA: Tricycle Press.

Lyubomirsky, S. (2001). Why are some people happier than others?: The role of cognitive and motivational processes in well-being. *Social Indicators Research, 56*(3), 239–249.

Lyubomirsky, S. (2008). *The how of happiness: A scientific approach to getting the life you want*. New York: Penguin.

Lyubomirsky, S., & Lepper, H. S. (1997). A measure of subjective happiness: Preliminary reliability and construct validation. *Social Indicators Research, 46*, 137–115.

Lyubomirsky, S., & Ross, L. (1997). Hedonic consequences of social comparison: A contrast of happy and unhappy people. *Journal of Personality and Social Research, 73*, 1141–1157.

McDermott, D., & Hastings, S. (2000). Children: Raising future hopes. In C. R. Snyder, (Ed.), *Handbook of hope* (pp. 185–199). San Diego, CA: Academic Press.

McDermott, D., & Snyder, C. R. (1999). *Making hope happen: A workbook for turning possibilities into realities*. Oakland, CA: New Harbingers Publications.

McMullen, K. (1996). *Noel the first*. New York: Michael di Capua Books.

Merriam, E. (1991). *The wise woman and her secret*. New York: Simon & Schuster Children's Publishing.

Park, N., Peterson, C., & Seligman, M. E. (2004). Strengths of character and well-being. *Journal of Social and Clinical Psychology, 23*(5), 603–619.

Oaklander, M. (2015). The science of bouncing back. *Time* http://time.com/3892044/the-science-of-bouncing-back/.

Parr, T. (2014). *It's okay to make mistakes*. New York: Little, Brown Books for Young Readers.

Pearpoint, J., O'Brien, J., & Forest, M. (1993). *PATH: A workbook for planning positive possible futures. Planning alternative tomorrows with hope for schools, organizations, business, families*. Toronto: Inclusion Press.

Peterson, C., & Seligman, M. E. (2004). *Character strengths and virtues: A handbook and classification*. Oxford University Press.

Pett, M., & Rubenstein, G. (2010). *The girl who never made mistakes*. Naperville, IL: Sourcebooks Jabberwocky.

Pink, D. H. (2011). *Drive: The surprising truth about what motivates us*. New York: Penguin NY.

Quinn, R. E. (2010). *Deep change: Discovering the leader within* (Vol. 378). John Wiley & Sons.

Quinn, R. E. (2015). *The positive organization: Breaking free from conventional cultures, constraints, and beliefs*. Berrett-Koehler. Oakland: CA

Rath, T. (2007). STRENGTHFINDER 2.0. New York: GALLUP.

Rath, T. (2009). *How full is your bucket? For kids*. N.A.: Gallup Press.

Rath, T. (2013). *Eat, move, sleep. how small changes lead to big changes*. N.A.: Missionday.

Rath, T. (2015). *Are you fully energized? The 3 keys to energizing your work and life*. N.A.: Silicon Guild.

Reynolds, P. (2014). *Going places*. New York: Atheneum Books for Young Readers.

Ritchhart, R., Church, M., & Morrison, K. (2011). *Making thinking visible: How to promote engagement, understanding, and independence for all learners*. New York: John Wiley & Sons.

Seligman, M. E. (2012). *Flourish: A visionary new understanding of happiness and well-being*. Simon and Schuster New York.

Shen, L., Hsee, C., Zhang, J., & Dai, X. (2011). Belittling can be flattering. *NA-Advances in Consumer Research, 38* pp. 170–172.

Solarz, P (2015). *Learn like a pirate: Empower your students to collaborate, lead and succeed*. San Diego, CA. Dave Burgess Consulting Inc.

Snyder, C. R. (2002). Hope theory: Rainbows in the mind. *Psychological Inquiry,* 13(4), 249–275.

Snyder, C. R., Harris, C., Anderson, J. R., Holleran, S. A., Irving, L. M.., Sigmund, S., T., & Harney, P. (1991). The will and the ways: Development and validation of the individual-differences measure of hope. *Journal of Personality and Social Psychology, 60,* 570–585.

Svitak, A. (2010, April 2). Adora Svitak: What adults can learn from kids. [Video file.] Retrieved from https://www.youtube.com/watch?v=V-bjOJzB7LY

Tough, P. (2012). *How children succeed: Grit, curiosity and the hidden power of character*. New York: Houghton Mifflin.

Tough, P. (2014). Who gets to graduate. *The New York Times* https://www.nytimes.com/2014/05/18/magazine/who-gets-to-graduate.html.

Tough, P. (2016). *Helping children succeed: Grit, curiosity and the hidden power of character*. New York: Houghton Mifflin.

Yamaguchi, K. (2011). *Dream big, little pig!* Naperville, IL: Sourcebooks, Jabberwocky.

Yeager, D. S., & Dweck, C. S. (2012). Mindsets that promote resilience: When students believe that personal characteristics can be developed. *Educational Psychologist, 47*(4), 302–314.

Yeager, J. M., Fisher, S. W., & Shearon, D. N. (2011). *Smart strengths: A parent-teacher-coach guide to building character, resilience, and relationships in youth*. New York: Kravis Publishing.

About the Authors

Dr. Kevin Sheehan Ed.D. is a tenured associate professor at Molloy College, where he has served on the faculty for over a decade. In 2013, Molloy College recognized Kevin with its Faculty Leadership Award for his work with children of poverty. In 2009, the New York State Council for Social Studies awarded Kevin the Distinguished Social Studies Educator Award for his efforts in preparing social studies teachers. Prior to his work at Molloy College, Kevin was the K-12 Social Studies Director for the Oceanside School District and was recognized as the outstanding supervisor for social studies by the New York State Council for Social Studies in 2002.

After receiving and publishing his doctorate from Hofstra, *Storm Clouds in the Mind*, Kevin has continued his research authoring several key articles on hope and has become a featured presenter on positive psychology topics across the nation. In another arena, influenced by positive psychology research that now defines his life's mission, Kevin is an internationally recognized lacrosse coach and has had a distinguished career in coaching. Kevin was inducted into the Long Island Metropolitan Branch of the US Lacrosse Hall of Fame in 2006 and the Oceanside Circle of Pride Hall of Fame in 2009.

Jessica Ryan has worked as a fourth-grade teacher in Lynbrook School District since 2007. Jessica graduated from the Molloy College Honors Program with a bachelor of science in elementary education concentrating in mathematics and was recognized as the outstanding graduate student in her class when she received her master's in elementary education. In 2013, Jessica began working as an adjunct professor at Molloy College, where she teaches the Advanced Mathematics Methods course to graduate education students. In her role as a Molloy professor, Jessica has developed a variety of creative summer teacher institutes and professional development courses for teachers.

Jessica was awarded the Nassau County Mathematics Teachers Association's Elementary Mathematics Teacher of the Year Award in 2012. In 2013, Jessica was named the Teacher of the Year by the 9/11 Tribute Center for her role involving students in community service. Jessica has been the recipient of numerous grants that have enabled her to develop innovative practices to meet the learning styles of diverse learners.

ABOUT THE CHAPTER AUTHORS

- **Angela Abend** is a nationally acclaimed elementary gifted education teacher in Oceanside, New York. Before teaching gifted education, Angela taught sixth grade and has been in the Oceanside School District for over 25 years.

- **Elisabetta Bavaro** is a dedicated lifelong learner who has worked as an enthusiastic elementary teacher in the Oceanside Union Free School District for 17 years. Betty has shared her insights and passion for social studies at both the intermediate and high school levels, and has been a regular presenter at the Long Island Council for the Social Studies, sharing innovative social studies practices since 2001.

- **Kathleen Nicoletti-Blake** is currently an elementary school teacher in the Oceanside School District. She has a degree in special education and a master's degree in literacy.

- **Amy Kanavy-Curry** has worked as an elementary teacher in Massapequa School District for the last 17 years. In 2015, Amy was honored to receive the Margaret Simon Award for Excellence in Elementary Social Studies Education from the Long Island Council for the Social Studies.

- **Dan Keegan**, an administrator at the Oceanside Middle School, was named the Long Island Social Studies Middle School Teacher of the Year in 2002 and the New York State Social Studies Middle School Teacher of the Year in 2003. Dan is currently directing a nationwide lab school partnership, which marries the C3's Inquiry Design Model with the Teaching Channel's TCH Team platform.

- **Jessica Keegan** is the elementary curriculum supervisor in the Oceanside, New York, School District. She is a nationally board-certified teacher with 15 years' elementary teaching experience.

- **Edward Kemnitzer** is currently the executive assistant for Technology Integration for Curriculum Support & Development for the Massapequa Public Schools. Ed is a former English teacher, curriculum associate, and assistant principal; he is dedicated to learning and is a cofounder of EdCamp Long Island.

- **Dr. Anthony J. Marino** is currently an elementary school teacher in the Oceanside Union Free School District and an adjunct professor at the School of Education, St. John's University. Anthony received the Molloy College Alumni Educator of Excellence Award in 2014.

- **Kelly Marzocchi** is an elementary school teacher in the Oceanside School District. She is currently working toward attaining a doctorate degree in instructional leadership at St. John's University.

- **AnnMarie Pagano** is currently going into her fourth year of teaching as the math teacher at the De La Salle School in Freeport, New York. In May 2016, she graduated with her master's degree in adolescent mathematics education from Molloy College, completing a thesis on the effects of grit on mathematics achievement.

- **Megan Pavlick** works as a special education teacher in the Massapequa School District and as an adjunct professor at Molloy College. In 2011, Megan's Student Council projects were recognized by Newsday, News12, and, in 2013, Megan attended the Project Zero Classroom at the Harvard Graduate School of Education.

- **Breanna Podmore** is entering her fourth year of teaching, currently as an eighth-grade living environment teacher at the Scholars Academy, a middle and high school in Rockaway Park Queens, New York. She earned her bachelor's degree at Molloy College in adolescent biology and special education, and will graduate with her master's degree in earth science from Stony Brook University in December 2016.

- **Danielle Rosenberg** is a second-year, third-grade special education teacher in Queens, New York. Danielle graduated Molloy College with a dual master's in 2015. Danielle has presented her elementary social studies units integrating hope and grit in the American Revolution with Dr. Sheehan at the Metropolitan New York City Social Studies Conference.

- **Kathleen Neagle Sokolowski** is an elementary school teacher in the Farmingdale School District. She is the codirector of the Long Island Writing Project, one of the coauthors of the Two Writing Teachers blog, and a recipient of the 2016 New York State English Council's Teacher of Excellence Award.

- **Faith Tripp** has had a variety of teaching experiences in grades K-12, and is an adjunct professor in the Graduate Department at Molloy College. In 2016, Faith was named as principal of the Chestnut Street School in the West Hempstead Union Free School District, where she currently serves as the director of English as a New Language.

- **Caitlin Verity** has been an elementary teacher in the Baldwin and Oceanside School Districts. She has found success through collaboration with others and enjoys professional development to further enhance her teaching expertise.
- **Megan Votke** has worked as an elementary teacher in Oceanside School District. After graduating from the State University College at Oneonta with a bachelor's degree in Childhood Education, Megan received a master's degree in literacy at Teachers College, Columbia University, and is currently working toward attaining a doctoral degree in instructional leadership at St. John's University.
- **Monica Zenyuh** is an elementary teacher in the Harborfields Central School District and an adjunct professor at Hofstra University. Monica is currently an ABD doctoral candidate at Hofstra University. Monica's dissertation involves creating a domain-specific grit instrument to measure mathematics grit and English-language arts grit.